D0103242

# UNCOVERING THE DOME

*Was the public interest served
in Minnesota's 10-year political brawl
over the Metrodome?*

by

## Amy Klobuchar

WAVELAND
PRESS, INC.

Prospect Heights, Illinois

For information about this book, write or call:

Waveland Press, Inc.
P.O. Box 400
Prospect Heights, Illinois 60070
(312) 634-0081

Cartoons courtesy of Richard Guindon.
Cover photo courtesy of Minneapolis Stadium
Commission.

*This is for mom and dad.*

I would like to express my sincere gratitude to Theodore Marmor, political science professor at Yale, for his careful guidance and perceptive criticism. While some members of his profession may have raised their eyebrows at the thought of supervising a project like this, his support was unflagging, his enthusiasm contagious. There is nothing more inspiring for a student.

Many of our interests are shaped in youth. I was raised in part on Sunday afternoon play-by-play's and Monday night color commentaries. My father's agonies in front of the television screen and pungent remarks on the shotgun offense left a lasting impression. In approaching that peculiar world, he advised a lively but inquiring mind. His teachings are not limited to athletics. He has spurred my interest in politics. He has challenged me to write. For his perspectives on the stadium as well as the much-heralded quality of life in Minnesota I'm very thankful.

There are three teachers at Yale I would like to acknowledge: Mihoko Suzuki, whose patient advice and moral support helped me to confront such mysteries as proper syntax and the word processor; Donald Faulkner, whose course gave me the confidence to write; and David Papke, who was constantly encouraging.

I am indebted to all of the people who gave their time in my research interviews. Without their thoughtful insights, "Uncovering the Dome" would have been a more difficult and less enjoyable undertaking.

Special thanks to Jon, Maggie, Meg and Liz. Although they've never been to Minneapolis, much less to a domed or undomed stadium there, they have persistently tolerated my efforts. Their friendship was, and is, invaluable.

**Amy Klobuchar**
**Chicago, 1982**

**"There's a time out down there on the field . . ."**
12-19-75
Minneapolis Star and Tribune

# THERE IT SQUATTED, PROUD, NEW AND DEFLATED . . .

It was wet, heavy snow. It was the kind of snow that gives shovelers slipped discs and clogs the best of snowblowers. By late evening the storm had toppled electrical lines in many rural and suburban areas. The people, being Minnesotans conditioned to snowy blitzkriegs, didn't panic. They are prepared for these situations. They have candles and campstoves. They have blankets and battery-run radios. Logs burned in fireplaces. Radio stations bleeped weather alerts. Neighbors peered out of frosted windows, watching the victims across the street futilely slip and slide, wheels grinding up and down the icy incline of their driveways.

Out of the windows of high-rise office buildings facing the southeastern corner of Minneapolis, wide-eyed dwellers witnessed an even more harrowing sight. In the southeastern corner of the city stands the brand-new, $55 million Hubert Humphrey Metrodome. With its gray coloring and billowy roof, the new home for the Minnesota Twins and Vikings looks something like a committee's compromise between a grounded flying saucer and a giant mushroom. The stadium's lumpy, teflon-coated nylon dome is air-supported — jetted up by thousands of pounds of steam pressure. The building is a credit to the wizardry of technology and state of the art engineering techniques. Yet those who watched the stadium on that snowy day in November were reminded that man, with all of his technical wisdom, still makes his bows to the whims of nature.

For on Nov. 18, 1981, the stadium's dome was undeniably, uncontrollably, unmercifully, sinking.

There were some who delighted in the dome's demise. After years of city council and state legislature debates, countless public hearings and committee deliberations, the dome had collapsed, among other reasons, for a lack of hot air. All that the legislative strategies, the myriad of law suits, and the fiery arguments had failed to accomplish was achieved by ten inches of snow.

Others were not amused by the stadium's predicament. Donald Poss, a former suburban city manager with an engineering background, was the executive director of the stadium commission. Poss has a reputation for getting projects done on time and under budget. He subscribes to the belief that government should be run like a business, with a minimum of bureaucratic mess. A storehouse of facts and figures, with a prompt response to every budget question, Donald Poss is the David Stockman of stadium construction.

In order to achieve a balanced budget on the project, Poss and his commission built a stadium without glamorous frills. They built it without air-conditioning and without the free office space offered to professional teams in other cities. They slashed unnecessary paint jobs and sliced the size of the press box. Poss was a shrewd negotiator, efficient and occasionally ruthless. But with all due respect to his counterpart in Washington, the stadium director's predictions held course. The project has been built on time and within budget. And although Poss has had some trickle-down problems of his own, they lack the severity of Stockman's experience. On November 18, 1981, the only thing trickling down upon Donald Poss was ten inches of snow.

"We had to call the fire department to get a ladder long enough so that the men could climb up and open the emergency plugs in the roof," he remembers now. "We just couldn't figure out why the snow wasn't melting. Later we learned that the gas company had forgotten to put in the winter valve. The summer orifice only supplied one-third the steam pressure of the winter one. So there was insufficient heat to keep the dome inflated."

The executive director and his troops spent the next two days steaming off the snow and reinflating the dome. The pressure inside the stadium was kept at an extremely high level in order to melt the remaining slush. Just when Poss was sure that he was home free, the high pressure caused one of the roof's panels to rip, sending a cascade of slush and ice chunks smack into the middle of left field. Wrote Minneapolis *Star* sportswriter Scott Papillon: "The Minnesota Twins won't even have to ship players back to the minors. They can just station them in left field and let them drift out to sea."

But despite the jeering and jabbing, the Metrodome survived. In what Poss describes as an "engineering marvel," the dome was reinflated within four days. The commission chartered a plane and picked up a new panel soon after the original panel punctured. Two days later the dome rose once again. It rebounded with a resiliency which characterized the stamina of its proponents for over a decade. Like the disciples of the Tennessee Valley Authority, statehood for Alaska, and other supposedly lost causes, the stadium people were tenacious. They were adaptable and persistent — not unlike Minnesotans in the wintertime.

# FOREWORD

Amy Klobuchar's prize-winning senior essay at Yale College is a highly readable book about Minnesota politics. Her subject — how a domed stadium came to be built in Minneapolis and below estimated costs — has all the elements of high drama and mundane detail. The story itself took years to unfold and the tale she tells is filled with routine and surprise, last-minute adjustments and longstanding antagonists. The site of discussion moved from the Capitol to boardrooms, from newspapers to polls, from public demonstrations to detailed hearings. And, in the course of it, the question of whether a stadium ought to be built got separated from the issue of where precisely it ought to be sited. That fateful separation is in itself an important part of the Klobuchar analysis. But there is much more — the way the topic emerged on the agenda of Minnesota politics, how groups organized and pressed their claims, and the extraordinary concern in Minnesota politics about the proper role of public authority in such an investment, and the limits of public financial responsibility.

The book supplies an intricate weaving of political theory and practical politics, the details of personality and individual effort set against the broader background of how issues are contested in Minnesota's public life. In large measure a well-told story, the book ends with the central questions of political evaluation. Did the building — and the siting — serve the larger public interest in Minnesota? Did the demands of public accountability get served by a stadium commission that eventually selected the Minnesota site? What accounts for the costs and timing of the completed project, especially in light of the troubled experiences other jurisdictions had in building football stadia at reasonable cost? Is Minnesota's experience a special case or does it foreshadow other examples of cooperation between private resources and public authority?

These are the topics this arresting book addresses. Essentially the culmination of an undergraduate education, this is a remarkable achievement for a young writer. It is of course a special pleasure when a teacher witnesses the flourishing of a student. The product, in this case, is a public benefit, a good story and a persuasive examination of a complicated episode in Minnesota's politics.

**Theodore R. Marmor**
**Professor of Public Health and Political Science**
**Yale University**

# CONTENTS

"If the Vikings and Twins left . . . we'd be well on our way to becoming a frozen Omaha." — Harvey MacKay's vision of life without field goals and RBIs.

# INTRODUCTION

In the early 1970s the Minneapolis City Council considered a proposal to build a professional sports stadium in the city of Minneapolis. Its deliberations ushered in a decade of frenzied politicking and a never-ending parade of stadium schemes. The coliseums came domed and undomed, urban and suburban, with retractable seats and retractable roofs. The City Council's proposed stadium, a 70,000-seat arena surrounded by a parking lot, was slated in 1973 as the new home for the Minnesota Vikings.

The Vikings, along with the Minnesota Twins baseball team, had been playing in Metropolitan Stadium in suburban Bloomington since the early 1960's. Both teams, but particularly the Vikings, were dissatisfied with the Bloomington facility. It had been built in 1955 when crowds were smaller, sports fans not yet coddled by weather-proofed stadiums, and television less omnipresent in the marketing of professional athletics. A relic of that vanished time of thirty-cent hotdogs and mud-stained uniforms, the Met was not congenial to briefly-dressed cheerleaders, posh business entertaining and elaborate television production. The

Minnesota Vikings, a well-established, profitable professional football team, were playing in one of the smallest and most antiquated sports arenas in the country. The Minnesota Vikings could undoubtedly be scoring touchdowns in a more lucrative, not to mention warmer, facility. The Minnesota Vikings were talking about leaving Minnesota.

By no means was the entire community alarmed by the Vikings' threats. Not all residents owed allegiance to the professional football team. If the Vikings wished to leave the Twin Cities, they were prepared to bid them good riddance. Some were vehemently opposed to the idea of the use of public subsidies for a private industry. Why should the people have to finance a multi-million dollar sports team, they asked. "If the jocks want a stadium," remarked one city council member, "then the jocks can pay for it."[1]

But the prevailing belief among city government officials and business leaders was that a stadium in Minneapolis would benefit downtown restaurants, hotels, and other commercial interests. According to one stadium crusader, the project would serve the public interest because it would generate jobs and economic development while insuring that professional sports remained in the area. "If the Vikings and Twins were to leave the Twin Cities," said Harvey MacKay, former president of the Minneapolis Chamber of Commerce, "We'd be well on our way to becoming a frozen Omaha."[2] The stadium would thus stand as a status symbol, a sign that Minneapolis was a thriving metropolitan area, on par with Dallas, Houston, New Orleans, and other expanding cities which could boast of sparkling new sports arenas.

When the city's effort to secure a new stadium failed in 1973, the issue scrambled onto the state legislative agenda. Two questions — where the stadium should be built and how it should be financed — spurred four years of emotional legislative debate and loquacious business lobbying. Eventually the Minnesota Legislature passed a "no site" bill which authorized the sale of bonds for the stadium, instituted a liquor tax to back the bonds, and stipulated spending limits on the stadium's construction. But the 1977 bill left the controversial issue of the arena's location to be decided by a seven-member citizens' commission appointed by the governor.

In Minnesota the stadium controversy was one of those issues on which practically everyone held an opinion. Not since the state's fight over the adoption of daylight savings time had there been such a continuous airing of publicly held views and passionate convictions. Spanning ten years of political history, the stadium shared the city's front page limelight with every beleaguered building from the Watergate to the Pentagon, with every controversial construction from the B-1 Bomber to the Concorde jet.

A journalist would call the stadium a "hot" issue. A political scientist might describe the controversy as a salient one to Minnesota's general public. Yet the people of Minnesota were never given the chance to express their preferences in a direct vote over the issue. Its opponents wondered how some could claim that the stadium was within the public interest, when, according to public opinion polls, the majority of the state's residents were against its construction. "If you asked people if they wanted a new stadium, they'd say yes," one legislative opponent remarked, "But if you asked them either if they wanted it in Minneapolis or if they wanted a stadium backed by public money, they'd say no . . . the people should have been given a chance to vote in a referendum."[3]

Advocates of the project spoke of the public interest in a different way. "I don't think that there was any question in anybody's mind that if there had been a referendum on the stadium it would have been defeated," recalled Steve Keefe, one of the state legislators who favored a downtown stadium. "But many people didn't understand that the Vikings would have left if they didn't get a new stadium. Nor did they fully understand the economic arguments for the downtown site."[4]

"Public opinion might have been against the stadium," conceded Louis DeMars, former president of the Minneapolis city council, "but that doesn't mean that politicians who favored the proposal worked against the public interest." DeMars believes politicians have to use their brains and good judgment to make a decision and after they've made that decision the record will show whether it was good or bad. "I don't think that elected officials are supposed to put their fingers in the air and see which way the wind is blowing," he said, "You can throw them out of office or not throw them out of office depending on how they perform. That's how democratic government serves the public interest."[5]

The public interest. Surely it is one of the most carelessly overused terms in political discourse.[6] Politicians use it to justify every engineering brainstorm from the building of massive bridges to the subsidization of lunar visits. Corporate heads are adept at spewing "public interest" rationalizations for anything from plant relocations to environmentally-hazardous production processes. The mere mention of the term evokes doubtful smirks and wearied sighs from even the mildest of cynics. Writes Brian Barry in *Political Argument:*

> It has become fashionable in some quarters to dismiss the concept of the "public interest" as devoid of content. Its use as a counter of public debate is said to be fraudulent, since there is no such thing as a "public interest," and it is claimed that if it has any social function it is merely that of casting an aura of legitimacy around decisions which are in fact the outcome of group pressures. But it makes good sense to suppose that there are interests common to all members of a community.[7]

Barry defines the public interest as those interests which people have in common as members of the public.[8] This definition echoes Rousseau, who believed that the purpose of government is to serve those interests which are shared by all people and that "it is on the basis of this common interest alone that society must be governed."[9]

Other political theorists have defined the "public interest" not as that common denominator of interests which the members of a society share, but rather as a reflection of the preferences of a majority of the individuals in the society. If, for instance, most voters favor a certain tax limitation (i.e. the Proposition 13 in California), then its adoption coincides with the public interest. While citizens may express their demands by voting, it is not the act itself which determines this aggregate interest. Rather it is the prevailing opinion which defines the public interest. Theorists such as Jeremy Bentham define the interest of a community as "the sum of the interests of the several members of the community who compose it."[10] Thus the public interest is identical to the greater sum of individual interests.

Yet a third theory holds that the public interest is a moral concept: It is viewed as a transcendental entity, a concept larger than life, not necessarily equivalent to the aggregate sum of individual interests. It is judged by values and roles such as "maximize human freedom," "promote justice," or "preserve stability."[11] "The good in the sphere of politics is justice," wrote Aristotle, "and justice consists in what tends to promote the common interest."[12]

The most penetrating minds in scholarship have failed to pronounce the final word on the concept which Justice Felix Frankfurter once described as ". . . that vague, impalpable, but all-controlling consideration, the public interest."[13] Yet the dispute over its precise meaning does not detract from the central role the "public interest" plays in political decision-making. It is a persistent sentinel of democracy for elected officials, goading them to remember in whose name they are acting. It means there is a common ground for promoting private interests and that much of the time those private interests are best served by policies which benefit the general public.

So what does all of this have to do with a domed sports stadium in Minneapolis? What is Aristotle doing in a fight over tail-gating? The story of the Minneapolis Metrodome, like the stories of a host of other public policies and projects in America, is a study in the politics of public interest. It is a story of how a project comes to be defined as within the public interest; why it becomes an object of governmental concern; how it weaves in and out of the political tapestry of group interests and individual ambitions.

The Metrodome is a case study, and thus it shares the shortcomings of other case studies. A sports stadium is a particular public project and Minneapolis is a particular city. Its government operates differently from governments in Chicago or Los Angeles or even neighboring St. Paul. The Minnesota legislature differs from other state governments. Concerns raised in local disputes differ from those which surface in the national political arena. Although ideological differences enter into local disputes, they do not produce the philosophical or moral clashes which characterized the country's struggle over civil rights legislation or the debate over the nation's involvement in the Vietnam War.

But a local case study does offer an opportunity to explore the way things work in American politics: the shifting coalitions and uncertain outcomes; the scattered interests and chaotic atmosphere; the differing conceptions of what serves the public interest. These are the questions the Metrodome posed.[15]

1. Why was this project defined as being within the public interest? How was government intervention justified?
2. How did the political process serve the public interest? How were conflicting demands articulated, legitimized and weighed?
3. Was the final outcome solely the result of electoral politics or was decision-making authority delegated to people who were not responsible to the voting public? How much did individual conceptions of the public interest affect the final outcome?
4. Was the government responsive to the public after the decision was made? Was the implementation of the project consistent with the original intent of the legislation?

A recurrent theme throughout this analysis will be the close interdependence between public and private interests. A government action is often considered contrary to the public interest simply because it benefits one or more private interests. Efforts motivated by profit do not preclude business from simultaneously making a contribution to the community. One way to reverse the economic blight which currently confronts many of America's cities would be through innovative public-private partnerships. But in order to forge these partnerships, the cities not only need viable business communities, but also assertive governments which cannot be manipulated by business interests.

This case illustrates how the public and private sectors can work together to produce an outcome acceptable to both forces, how business incentives and efficient market techniques can be incorporated into the workings of government. The way in which the government handled the stadium issue — the demands and expectations placed on the business community, the emphasis on careful, long-term planning — demonstrates how well government can operate in Minnesota. The state is known nationally for its public-private partnerships. While the business community traditionally rails against the tax climate in Minnesota, it has willingly entered into a cordial relationship with local and state planners on a wide range of projects which have proven beneficial to both private and public interests. It would be more difficult to implement this type of partnership in larger, more politically volatile communities. Yet the "Minnesota model" serves as an example of how this partnership can be successful.

One might conclude that only a person with either an all-consuming interest in professional sports or a fixation with stadium construction would choose to pursue the evolution of the Metrodome. The author pleads not guilty to both charges. The value of this story lies in the opportunity it provides to explore the fiber of American politics. Like many of the political disputes in this country, from the siting of an airport to that of a hospital, the fight over the Metrodome was a fight over a project's location. Like an array of hard-fought battles over taxes and publicly financed projects, the stadium controversy was also forever entangled with the question of who would pay.

A case study such as this enables one to look at these questions through a magnified lens, to disentangle the threads which form the fabric of American politics. Here is the pushing and pulling of competing interest groups, the convictions and political posturing, the clamoring, the clashing, the noise.

This is not an idealized civics book version of how things *should* work in American politics. This is a story of how they *do* work.

# 1

# THE STADIUM: 1971-1973

## Inside the Purple Palace

A visit to the Minnesota Vikings' newly built, corporate-chic,
practice facility and business complex must be disillusioning to
anyone harboring memories of professional football as it was 50
years ago. Gone are those primeval days when pro football was
"only a game," when players wore leather head coverings and
top stars were paid less than $200 per game, when purchasing a
franchise cost $50 and owning a team was more of a hobby than
it was an investment. Like the Orange, N.J. Tornadoes (NFL
'29), the Duluth Eskimos (NFL '23-'27), and the Staten Island
Stapletons (NFL '29-'32), those happy-go-lucky yesteryears are
nearly forgotten, nourished now only by nostalgia trippers.

Welcome to the 1980's: an era of six-figure player salaries,
electronic scoreboards, and flashy halftime shows; an age when
the same stuff they use to coat the players' helmets augments the
nose-cones of atomic missiles; when television dictates everything
from the colors of the uniforms to the scheduling of time-outs;
when four of the nine most popular television shows of all time
are Super Bowls — a game for which a half-minute commercial

costs $345,000.

Owning a football team is no longer the recreation of a handful of sporting zealots. It is a thriving multi-million dollar industry. And like any other thriving, multi-million dollar industry, it needs a home worthy of its stature. The Vikings' headquarters, which owner Max Winter commissioned in 1981, is similar to the business headquarters of prestigious corporations across the country — with large, plush offices, an expansive and comfortable lobby, a hushed, dignified atmosphere which whispers of important dealings and profitable investments.

"Winter Park" differs from other commercial offices in at least three respects, however. Instead of planting rose bushes or installing fountains to enhance the aesthetic value of the building's surrounding grounds, Max Winter has fashioned a 100-yard practice field, complete with goal-posts and a retractable dome. In the building's basement, where some businesses might house a storage room or employee cafeteria, sprawls a locker room of mammoth proportions. And while other offices may be set in tasteful blues or grays or shades of brown and beige to reflect the stately nature of their businesses, the Vikings have chosen to decorate their offices less subtly, in a color which serves as the trademark for their company. It is purple. And it is relentless.

From the carpeting to the sofas to the wastepaper baskets, it is purple. A brilliant purple pervades the drinking mugs, the plant holders, the violets which dangle from the secretaries' office windows. Even the lamps which illuminate this gilded place are propped up on shellacked purple-and-gold football helmets.

Residing in this purple palace are those who rule over the Vikings' empire — among them owner Max Winter and General Manager Mike Lynn. Winter is the one who built the new headquarters and was instrumental in building the team. An Austrian immigrant whose first venture into the sports business was a part-ownership in a four-lane bowling establishment, he was one of five hopeful businessmen who together risked the $600,000 to acquire a professional football franchise for Minnesota in 1961. "I came into the NFL when there were only twelve owners," the 77-year-old promoter said in a recent interview.

"For a guy who used to sell papers on the street, it has been a tremendous ego trip . . . you get in an elevator at the Waldorf Astoria, and someone might say, 'Aren't you Max Winter of the Minnesota Vikings?' Not many people would recognize the president of U.S. Steel or of AT & T."[1]

Although Winter's business doesn't qualify as a "Fortune 500" company like U.S. Steel or AT & T, the comparison is a valid one. The Vikings' organization is a profit-maximizing enterprise. Its primary goal — its raison d'etre — is to make money. Like any well-run company, the organization has its hierarchy of management positions. General Manager-Vice President Mike Lynn is at the top of that hierarchy. After an unsuccessful effort to acquire an NFL franchise for Memphis, Tennessee, Lynn was hired as General Manager of the Vikings in 1974.

Not much can ruffle the General Manager's easy-going demeanor or sour his sociable grin, but when Mike Lynn is confronted by something he sees as an obstacle to the workings of his company, he can be as ruthless as any of the Norse warriors for which the team is named.

Metropolitan stadium was such an obstacle.

"Is it true that you once referred to the Bloomington stadium as 'a piece of crap?' " asks a visitor perched upon one of the purple chairs which adorn the General Manager's office.

"I really called it something else," responds the General Manager, "only they wouldn't print it."[2]

## Grumblings from the Gridiron

The year is 1971. The Minnesota Vikings have been playing at Metropolitan Stadium in suburban Bloomington for a decade. The Met was built for the Minneapolis Millers baseball team in 1955 and expanded for major league sports in 1961 and 1965. The sight lines for football are poor. The bleacher section in the end zone is supported by blocks and girders. The grass is frequently frozen and sometimes invisible, particularly when it is buried beneath a foot of snow. But there are other considerations besides unsuitable vantage points, makeshift benches, and primitive playing conditions which make the Met undesirable for the Vikings franchise. The 48,700-seat arena is one of the smallest in professional football. Opposing teams who receive a proportion of the game's profits when they play at the stadium are not pleased with the relatively skimpy sums the Met generates. Neither are the Minnesota Vikings. In addition to the stadium's limited revenue-raising capabilities, the team is unhappy with the Met's locker rooms, press box, scoreboard, and other inadequacies which they say make the stadium miserable for play and practice.

There is also the question of pride. Professional sports is a glamorous business. In the words of the Vikings' owner, it is a "tremendous ego builder."[3] And Metropolitan Stadium was almost made to deflate any sports promoter's ego. As though it isn't painful enough to have come in second in last year's Super Bowl, the Vikings have to play in a second-rate house.

Try if you can to empathize with the team's management. Imagine that you have invited out-of-town friends to your house for the weekend. Minutes before your guests are to arrive, your floor becomes engulfed by a quagmire of mud and slush. Your guests fumble and slide, wrenching their knees and twisting their forearms. Your party is denounced as an abysmal disaster. And as if your pride hasn't suffered enough, you hear that Howard Cosell has announced on national television that some of your guests have been removed from their seats for fear of frostbite.

Wouldn't you be tempted to call a new real estate agent?

If the Bloomington stadium is bad for games, it is worse for practice. Until the Twins' season is over, the Vikings have had to practice in a variety of small pastures and public playgrounds, including an annual exile to a park in St. Paul which is also used for exercising dogs from the animal rescue league. The team's offices are cramped, their training equipment in a state of perpetual motion, their players' hands and feet never far from numb immobility.

Yet the perils of the Met are not nearly as bothersome to the Vikings' fans as they are to the Vikings' management. The stadium's surrounding prairies of asphalt provide a much-venerated picnic ground for pregame tailgating and postgame carousing. Tailgating may be a national pastime, but in Minnesota they do it with a zeal unmatched in other parts of the country. The frozen weather gives the northern fans an excuse to pour just a little more rum in their hot cider, or to toss a couple extra shots of schnapps in their hot chocolate.

A prerequisite for this parking lot frolicking is an automobile. Unless you ride a special football game charter bus from one of the area hotels or bars there is no public transportation to Vikings or Twins games. This lack of public bus service has little effect on Vikings attendance, as professional football attracts a middle to high income clientele. But baseball appeals to a notably different crowd — a crowd which is often dependent upon public transportation. "I challenge people to try and get a bus to the Met for a Twins game," says Twins Vice President Clark Griffith. "Met stadium is totally dependent on the use of private automobiles for its attendance. That eliminates a lot of poorer, younger and older people from attending Twins games."[4]

Yet in 1971 the Twins oppose the proposal for a new domed stadium because it calls for a football-only sports arena. With one Super Bowl behind them and another one almost certainly on the way, some claim that the Minnesota Vikings have brought a vitality and excitement to the area which even exceeds the electricity generated by the Twins' 1965 World Series appearance or the Minneapolis Lakers basketball team's five NBA championship victories. Not since the publishing of Longfellow's "Hiawatha" has a Minnesota phenomenon aroused more national notoriety. Not since the first crowning of the "Land of Lakes" butter queen has an event instilled as much local pride and patriotism.

The logic goes something like this: any state which can boast of a team known across the country as the "Purple People-Eaters," a team which has seen, if not touched, the grail of the Super Bowl, is a state worthy of national acclaim. Any team which can thrust that state into the national limelight deserves to play in a major league arena. And any major league arena which houses this first-rate team should certainly be located in a city

5

which is struggling for first-rate recognition, a city striving for national acceptance and economic enhancement.

Enter the city of Minneapolis.

## The "Mini-Apple

"When people think of San Francisco, Las Vegas, or New York, they think of that city's image," says Roger Toussaint, director of sales and marketing of the Minneapolis Convention and Tourism Commission. "The problem with Minneapolis is that it has an image of being cold."[5] The city of Minneapolis strikes a sour note for some — it is one of those places you visit only when you have to. Yet others, who see in it the excitement and attraction of the "Big Apple," without the accompanying crime, noise, and unmanageable size, have dubbed it the "Mini-Apple." To them it is a midwestern Shangri-la: a place where no one lives more than five minutes away from a lake, where population density is low and unemployment is significantly below the national average. According to a currently popular book of predictions, by 1999 the United States government will no longer be located in Washington D.C. It will have moved to Minneapolis.[6]

Even the most obsessed Minneapolitans should balk at this forecast.

But they will preach that there is more to their city than cows, cornfields, and contentment. Along with neighboring St. Paul, the city has been ranked number one by the National Urban Institute for overall quality of life, based on indicators including housing, income, education, the environment, and recreation. Residents have established a robust community despite an average winter low of four degrees and an average annual snowfall of forty-two inches. The Twin Cities have sprung from frontier mill towns to cultural centers, the home of 39 playhouses and theaters and 37 art galleries, including the world-renowned Guthrie Theater and Walker Arts Center.

A century ago the Twin Cities' economy revolved around the lumber and flour industries. Today the cities house the headquarters of 12 of the "Fortune 500" companies, including such diverse national firms as Control Data, Honeywell, General Mills, Pillsbury, 3M and Cargill Inc. The computer industry is especially important to the area's economy. Yet unlike Detroit and the auto industry, or Pittsburgh and the steel companies, the economies of Minneapolis and St. Paul have never been dominated by a single industrial base.

Government at the city and state levels is characterized by a high degree of citizen participation. The Scandinavian and German immigrants, with their demand for open government and their belief in an educated and involved citizenry, brought a tradition of good government to the area. Minnesota invariably has one of the highest voter turnouts in state and national elections. Government is generally balanced: Neither party has been dominant in either state or national politics for an extended period of time. With a reputation for progressive politicians — Hubert Humphrey, Eugene McCarthy, and Walter Mondale — and progressive legislation, Minnesota has been a leader in such national movements as those to guarantee the rights of women, minorities and especially the American Indians. The state relies heavily on the income tax rather than property and sales taxes to finance public services and it has one of the highest and most progressive income tax rates in the country.

Exposed to a minimal amount of political corruption, Minnesota voters do not normally share the cynical view of government held by citizens of other states who have been conditioned by years of political scandal. For the most part voters in Minnesota trust the people they choose to represent them. While residents in some states rely on referenda as a means to ensure that the public's will is legislated, Minnesota has never had a tradition of citizens' referenda. Government is accepted as a legitimate means of decision-making. "People in Minneapolis are open-minded about government," says Arthur Naftalin, former Mayor of Minneapolis and now a professor at the University of Minnesota. "Government is not considered to be an enemy of the private sector, instead it is an aid, a helper. There is a spirit here that government does not necessarily have to be onerous."[7]

Yet simply because the people generally trust their elected

officials does not, of course, ensure that those politicians will always govern wisely. In 1982, for instance, the state of Minnesota was faced with a $300 million budget deficit. Caused in part by inflation, the large deficit was also the result of poor economic predictions by the state administration, tax cuts, and the use of a disputed tax-indexing system.

And like any other state, Minnesota has its share of political skeletons rattling in the basement. The long-standing rivalry between Minneapolis and St. Paul is, according to Minnesota AFL-CIO President David Roe, a "counterproductive" force which has "been going on for years and will probably continue for many more." According to Roe, "It is present in the labor movement, in the business community, in the banking and insurance businesses, and in the government."[8] As the local prairie philosopher Garrison Keillor put it, "the difference between St. Paul and Minneapolis is the difference between pumpernickle and Wonder bread."[9] St. Paul has the image of being more ethnic and less innovative than its sister-city Minneapolis, which is characterized as businesslike and glamorous compared with St. Paul. Reporter Finlay Lewis of the Minneapolis *Star and Tribune* describes the relationship between the two cities during the mid-40s.

> The term "Twin Cities" seemed a misnomer in those days: to cross the Mississippi River from St. Paul to Minneapolis — or vice versa — required an act of will. It wasn't that the distance was so great (it wasn't) or that the street car connections were so complicated (they were). It was that the cities were so different. They didn't encourage visits back and forth. St. Paul was older, stagnant, smaller, Catholic, conservative, tradition-bound. Minneapolis was growing, exciting, changing, dynamic, Lutheran, Scandinavian. St. Paul was darkly suspicious of its neighbor. Minneapolis, when it bothered to notice, glanced back across the river with contempt.[10]

Time has served to mitigate the intense rivalry between the two cities. "The rivalry is given more attention than it probably deserves," says former Mayor Naftalin. "Much of it falls into the realm of myth and poetry . . . Yet there are vestiges of the rivalry in state politics today. It certainly played a role in the stadium controversy."[11]

## A City Makes a Proposal

"DOWNTOWN WOOS VIKINGS WITH PROMISE OF HOME," reads the Minneapolis *Tribune*'s front-page headline on October 3, 1971. The opening paragraph contained a quote from Max Winter. "A lot of people are making love to us," said the Vikings' owner, "but no one has proposed."[12]

In 1971 the Vikings were looking for a new home. Members of the Minneapolis City Council were talking about building them one. This wasn't the first time that the idea had been kicked around in the city government. They were considering it as far back as 1954.

In the early fifties many Twin Cities' business and government leaders were trying to entice big league football and baseball to the state of Minnesota. But first they needed a stadium. There were a couple of proposed Minneapolis sites, but members of the St. Paul Council refused to participate in the venture if the stadium were to be built in Minneapolis.

The siting of Metropolitan stadium was a compromise between government leaders in St. Paul and Minneapolis. By constructing a facility in the "neutral" suburb of Bloomington, the cities' officials hoped to avoid additional friction between the two communities. But in the end the city of St. Paul did not assist in the financing of the stadium. The Met was built with general obligation bonds backed by the credit of the city of Minneapolis. The Metropolitan Sports Area Commission, composed of four Minneapolis representatives, one representative from Bloomington, and one from the neighboring suburb of Richfield, was created to operate the stadium.

When the stadium was built in 1955, Bloomington was indeed a "neutral" suburb. A rustic community with a population of about 10,000, the village carried little if any political or economic clout within the state. But in the next five years the population of Bloomington soared to 50,000 people. Housing developments, sleek thoroughfares, and shiny office buildings accompanied the rapid migration of people to suburb from city. Hotels, bars and restaurants burgeoned around the Bloomington-located Twin Cities airport and nearby Metropolitan stadium.

Members of the Minneapolis City Council had never been enamored of the Bloomington stadium. They didn't like the idea of using their city's credit to build a stadium out in the suburbs. They became even more irritated when the economically expanding community of Bloomington (the village became a city in 1960) refused to shoulder the cost of the stadium's upkeep. Understandably, a village as small as Bloomington was in 1955 could never have backed the bonds which were originally sold to build the stadium. But Minneapolis officials felt that as a growing suburb it should pay a part of the stadium's maintenance and renovation.

"Minneapolis figured that eventually Bloomington would contribute something to the stadium's upkeep. But instead of contributing money, they asked for more money," recalls labor leader David Roe, a prominent figure in the stadium controversy who was involved with the issue as far back as 1954. "The suburb assessed the city of Minneapolis, through the stadium, for all utilities. For a couple of years Bloomington even refused to provide police service for games. They even requested that a three percent admissions tax be put into the general fund of Bloomington."[13]

At one point the city of Bloomington condemned the left field bleachers in an attempt to have Minneapolis build permanent seats. Roe regards this demand as a serious mistake on the part of Bloomington officials. "At that time if the Bloomington people would have acted constructively they would have said, 'hey . . . we'll float a million or two dollars worth of bonds for 10,000 more permanent seats in order to put the capacity up around 60,000,' " says Roe. "If they would have done that then there wouldn't have been many sound arguments for building a new stadium. The teams would most likely still be playing out in Bloomington."[14]

By 1971 the Metropolitan Sports Commission came up with a

new plan to expand and remodel the Met. It called for the city of Minneapolis to once again use its credit so that the commission could borrow money to finance the renovation. Several Minneapolis aldermen expressed angry opposition to the idea of spending any more money to promote suburban Bloomington.[15] City Council members had watched the development of the "Bloomington strip," a string of hotels and restaurants which surround the airport and stadium. They had witnessed the exodus of city dwellers and city businesses to Bloomington and other surrounding suburbs. Why should we use the city's money to subsidize a hot shot, ungrateful ex-cowtown, they asked. Why not use the city's money to help the city? Minneapolis needed the economic development that the stadium could generate. It wanted more jobs and a larger tax base. It could certainly use the national attention.

The Minneapolis Planning and Development Department had not been enthusiastic about the idea two years earlier, however. A 1969 staff report entitled "New Options for Downtown Problems" warned that "sports facilities on a large scale (stadium, etc.) will cause too much traffic and parking problems if located within the Downtown. Current facilities in Bloomington may be adequate."[16] Yet City Council members were willing to put up with some Sunday afternoon traffic jams in exchange for the economic and psychological benefits they thought the city could accrue from a downtown stadium. They tried to ease the parking problem by considering a novel stadium plan which would surround the arena with parking spirals.

The ramps would be shaped like a doughnut, with the stadium filling the hole. Originated by Minneapolis architect Robert Cerny, the idea grew out of the city's plans for a $10 million parking ramp to be built over the Third Avenue distributor in the northwestern corner of the city. With seating for 65,000 and parking spots for 5,100, the project was priced at $49 million. The ramp was to be used for football fans on weekends and downtown shoppers and employees during the week. Since many of the buildings around the site were old warehouses, apartment buildings, and run-down rooming houses, the project would not disrupt neighborhoods or businesses. The stadium was also in accord with city development plans — the parking garage was to be built even if the stadium was not.

Although the Vikings' lease with the Metropolitan Sports Commission was to expire in 1975, City Council members were concerned with the stadium not so much as a vehicle to keep the Vikings, but rather as a tool to spark economic development. The Minneapolis City Council, like other city councils across the country, was development-oriented. By the early 1970s, the Twin Cities area had become the nation's 15th largest metropolitan area. It was exceeded by only two larger metropolitan areas in rate of growth over the 1960's. The city of Minneapolis had just witnessed the development of the Nicollet Mall — a tree-lined, pedestrian shopping mall running through the center of the city — and the building of the Government Center. The city was ripe for an exciting new project like the stadium. City Coordinator Thomas A. Thompson estimated that the stadium would "spur $200 million in nearby development and bring in an increase of five to six million annually in business downtown."[17]

In February of 1971 the Minneapolis City Council and the Downtown Council agreed to split the $25,000 expense for further study of Cerny's parking lot-stadium proposal. The Downtown Council, which represented approximately 200 downtown retailers, bankers, building managers and small shop owners, was initially divided on the issue. Eventually a majority of the Council's members warmed to the idea, deciding that the stadium proposal was at least worthy of the $12,500 commitment for a feasibility study.

The feasibility report recommended that the $49 million project be built and insisted that it could be financed entirely out of revenues with no burden on the taxpayer. Both government and business leaders wanted absolute safeguards to prevent the financing of the stadium from turning into the debacle encountered by taxpayers in other cities. In 1971 a number of stadium horror stories were circulating. The public had already paid $9 million for Cincinnati's Riverfront stadium. The arena, built for football and baseball, was falling about $1 million short of meeting its $2.8 million yearly payment. The Three Rivers Stadium in Pittsburgh — also a two-team stadium — was losing money. Some $6 million had been collected from city taxpayers for streets and other improvements related to Busch Memorial Stadium in St. Louis. Houston property owners were taxed $31 million of the Astrodome's $45 million cost.[18]

Minneapolis government leaders were committed to finding a financing plan which would present no risk to city taxpayers, a plan which called for substantial aid from the business community and a long-term, high-paying lease from the Vikings. In January of 1972 negotiations began between the city, the business community, and the Vikings management.

The Minneapolis leaders were not the only ones who had entered the stadium sweepstakes, however. In 1972 the Minnesota Vikings were bombarded with a barrage of stadium offers. Everyone was courting the Vikings.

The University of Minnesota wanted the team. The school had installed artificial turf and improved the location of 20,000 seats in the University's Memorial stadium, better known by student-jocks as "the brickyard." Some interpreted this renovation as a move to attract the Vikings.

Bloomington wanted the Vikings. Leaders of the suburb, along with neighboring Richfield, were talking about building and financing a stadium just east of Metropolitan stadium at a cost of $10 to $10.5 million. Bloomington also proposed less expensive plans to either remodel the Met or build a new football stadium adjacent to the Met — thus saving the cost of land acquisition. But suburban officials conceded that neither of the latter proposals would be viable because both required the cooperation of the Minneapolis representatives on the Sports Commission.

St. Paul wanted the Vikings. The city made a late entry into the stadium derby when Mayor Lawrence Cohen came up with a plan for a $60 million, 80,000-seat domed football stadium and mass transit terminal to be built on twenty acres west of the State Fair racetrack and within a short distance of the University's St. Paul farm campus.[19]

Then there was the diplomatic proposal. Some neutrality-conscious souls wanted the stadium to be positioned so that one goal line would lie in Minneapolis, the other in St. Paul. This way points could be scored in both jurisdictions.

By the fall of 1972 so many stadium alternatives had been proposed that one Minneapolis *Star* columnist jested that the state had "finally reached that utopian plane of the democratic dream: one-man, one-stadium . . . If all of the plans are as dynamically sound as their sponsors insist," he wrote, "and the Vikings begin playing their exhibition games in March, it will be theoretically possible for each Viking fan to watch professional football in his own stadium."[20]

Perplexed by the proliferation of stadiums, the Vikings' board of directors commissioned the Stanford Research Institute to do a survey of their 13,000 season ticket-holders. The thrust of the survey was to find out whether the season ticket-holders preferred Met Stadium or the downtown proposal. Of the 7,801 people who answered the survey, 58 percent said that they were in favor of the Vikings remaining at Metropolitan stadium and 42 percent wanted the team to move to the proposed Minneapolis stadium. One-third of the pro-downtown respondents indicated that they would prefer the Met if some improvements were made.[21]

Yet the club's choice of sites was not anchored to the wishes of the season ticket-holders. It was to be decided by the Vikings' board of directors. The five-member board was fairly certain that the regular customers would buy tickets regardless of stadium location.

Each of the five directors had one vote. Bernie Ridder, chairman of the board and St. Paul newspaper publisher, was in favor of either enlarging the Met or building a new stadium in Bloomington. Ole Haugsrud of Duluth agreed with Ridder. Vikings President Max Winter and H.P. Skoglund, an insurance executive, were in favor of the Minneapolis site. The 2-2 tie left Vikings President E.W. Boyer with the deciding vote.

In December of 1972 the Bloomington and Minneapolis proposals were presented to the Board of Directors. Boyer was distressed by the vagueness of the Bloomington plans. While he claimed that he would rather have the Vikings playing out at the

Met, he conceded that the stadium simply wasn't large enough. "They just talked in generalities," he said of the Bloomington officials, "and we can't put peoples' butts in generalities. We've got to have seats."[22] E.W. Boyer cast the crucial vote for Minneapolis.

Soon after the Vikings negotiated an agreement with the city. The team was required to pay a rental fee of 15 percent of gross ticket sales. The fee was to be reduced (but not to less than 11 percent) if revenues from sources other than the Vikings exceeded 1.15 million dollars annually. The city would receive all revenues from concessions, advertising and the 4,000-car parking ramp that was to surround the stadium. The Vikings were to play a minimum of 95 home games in the stadium in any ten-year period within 30 years from the time the stadium was ready for occupancy. Should the Vikings move to another stadium before the contract ended, the club would pay the city "liquidated damages" of $600,000 a year to help dissolve the outstanding debt. The club would not be held liable for players' strikes or an "act of God or a public enemy" which might reduce the number of games played in a season.[23]

With the contract set, it was time for the City Council to vote on the proposal. On December 15, 1972, the Minneapolis *Tribune* reported that of the 13 aldermen, six favored the stadium, three were against its construction, and four were undecided.[24] The undecided council members were particularly concerned with the burden the stadium might pose to city taxpayers. The plan called for the sale of general obligation bonds to finance the construction. While the bonds themselves would not jeopardize taxpayers, it was the stadium's operating expenses which worried the aldermen. City Coordinator Thompson estimated the expenses for the stadium at about $2 million a year and income at about $2.2 million.[25] But if the predictions failed to hold up, if the expenses exceeded the revenue and there wasn't enough money to make the principal and interest payments on the bonds, Minneapolis taxpayers would have to pay the deficit through their property taxes.

Such a situation would certainly be sticky for council members who wanted to be re-elected. The aldermen needed to find a safeguard so that their constituents would never have to bear the cost of a possible deficit. Before they would accept the proposal they wanted a promise from the city's business community — an ironclad guarantee that if there was a deficit the business people would pay it.[26]

In the early months of 1973 the focus of the controversy shifted away from the Vikings and away from Bloomington. It was now the bankers' and merchants' turn to make a proposal.

## A Business Tradition

"The most important things in this town have happened at the initiative of the business community, not of government,"[27] said Minneapolis Mayor Donald Fraser in a 1981 interview. The city's Nicollet Mall, the Guthrie Theater, the Orchestra Hall, the 70 enclosed second-story skyways which link buildings on fourteen blocks — almost every city improvement has been planned and paid for by the business community. Minneapolis is the first city in the country to start a "five percent" club. Each year 45 companies give five percent of their taxable income (the maximum that federal regulations allow as a corporate income tax deduction) to charitable or civic causes.

The active role that the Minneapolis private sector has played in helping government to meet community needs has aroused national attention and esteem. The Mott Foundation sponsors an annual conference at which business, government, and labor leaders from across the country gather in the city to discuss the workings of public-private partnerships. Baltimore and Louisville now have "five percent" clubs, and six corporations in Alabama have organized one on a statewide basis. Kansas City, Seattle, Oakland, Phoenix and Washington D.C. all have "two percent" clubs. Yet the current national average for corporate giving is still approximately one percent.[28]

One of the reasons why Minneapolis has had such a success with its public-private partnership is that with a population of 368,000, the city is small compared with many metropolitan areas. "Minneapolis isn't as layered and formal as other larger cities. People get to know each other here," remarked John Cowles Jr., owner of the Minneapolis *Star* and *Tribune,* "Now if you don't know each other you're likely to assume that the other guy has a hostile or adverse motive," says Cowles. "But if you know the guy, you can just call him up and say, 'What the hell do you think you're doing?' or 'Tell me about this, I don't understand.' That's how it works here."[29]

In addition to being fairly small, the city's population is strikingly homogeneous. A 1980 census showed that the Twin Cities metropolitan area's population of about two million had less than five percent blacks, Indians, Chicanos and southeast Asians. With such a low minority population, Minneapolis lacks the ethnic diversity which characterizes other American cities. People tend to come from similar backgrounds and they also share similar values, making it easier for business and government to pursue common objectives.

Minneapolis business people are proud of what private enterprise has accomplished in the city. This pride and sense of community helps to create a relatively trusting relationship between business and government. "Minneapolis behaves much more like a small town than other cities its size," says Steve Keefe, a former state senator who represented a Minneapolis district. "The Minneapolis business community is very interested and active in the development of downtown. They do things that are not typical of other areas."[30]

Keefe, who now serves on a Minneapolis Chamber of Commerce task force on state issues, cites the Chamber's role in the 1981 state budget cutbacks as an example of the positive relationship between the public and private sectors. "The president of the Minneapolis City Council called the president of the Chamber of Commerce and said that the state budget cuts could cause severe problems for the city. He asked the Chamber for help," recalls Keefe. "And the Chamber of Commerce, whose position it is that government should spend less, etc., has spent a lot of time to help the city deal with its financial problems. This is not the sort of thing that happens in other cities," he notes. "In St. Paul, for example, the Chamber of Commerce is demanding tax slashes and it seems that they could care less about what happens to the city.''[31]

It is more than size and homogeneity which help to foster the sense of understanding between government and business in Minneapolis. It also has something to do with the patterns which have developed over the years and with the people who have forged them. The city's "five percent" standard, for instance, was initiated by two Minneapolis businessmen in the late 1930's, when the IRS adopted a law which allowed corporations to give up to five percent of their income to charity. Not many businesses took advantage of the tax break. But in Minneapolis, Gene Nelson Dayton, owner of Dayton's Department store, and John Cowles Sr., owner of the city's morning and evening newspapers, adopted the standard soon after the law was passed. According to John Cowles Jr., the newspapers' present owner, Gene Nelson Dayton liked the idea because he had grown up in the Presbyterian church where he tithed (gave ten percent to the church). To Dayton the contribution was an extension of his religious commitment. Cowles' father adopted the standard because he viewed the contribution as "enlightened self-interest." John Cowles Jr. shares his father's belief that "if you give to the community and the community improves, then anyone living or working in the community (including the giver and his employees and customers) has benefited.''[32]

Fifty years later, the Star & Tribune Company has expanded, and Cowles directs his father's paper, along with holdings that include several other daily papers, radio and television stations. "Dayton's" is no longer a single department store, but a huge national corporation, with a chain of department stores, discount houses, specialty stores, and real estate companies. As the businesses have been passed down from generation to generation, so has the business tradition of public-spirited activity and charitable contributions. "An awful lot of things get started when just one or two people decided to take a chance and try something," says Cowles, "and when it works, the next time around a few more people copy it and pretty soon you have a pattern going in the community.''[33]

## The Mayor and his Masterplan

Given the established pattern of business involvement in the city's public-oriented projects, it was no surprise that Minneapolis City Council members expected the business community to underwrite part of the stadium's cost. Nor was it surprising that the business community responded to their demands. In early 1973, John Cowles Jr. offered to have the Minneapolis Star & Tribune Company assume 25 percent of a $600,000 business guarantee against any losses that might result from the proposed downtown stadium. Later it was reported that the business pledge to pay up to $600,000 of losses each year was to be divided roughly as follows: Dayton-Hudson and the Star & Tribune each pledged about 20 percent of the total; Investor's Diversified Services between 10 and 15 percent; Northwest and First National Bank would each pay about 10 percent; the remaining portion was to be divided among the major utilities and smaller companies.[34]

In addition to the business guarantee, city council members created a special tax assessment district, composed of Minneapolis businesses, to further protect the taxpaying public from the burden of any cost overruns. If expenses exceeded the $600,000 per year business guarantee, then the deficits would be spread proportionally against downtown businesses as a tax. Most Council members were confident that this safeguard would provide a net large enough to protect the public from any debts the stadium might incur. By a ten to three vote the aldermen passed the stadium proposal.

This was the scenario on February 6, 1973: The Minnesota Vikings were ready to pick up their cleats and head out to a new stadium in Minneapolis. The Minneapolis business community was enthusiastic about the proposal, pledging to bear the costs of any possible deficits. The Minneapolis City Council had endorsed the plan, annointing the stadium with political legitimacy. It appeared that the project's proponents had contrived an infallible formula for the construction of a new stadium in Minneapolis.

It was put together by many resourceful people. But it crumbled before the unpredictable energies of one man outside the establishment of the city of Minneapolis — the Mayor of Minneapolis, Charles Stenvig.

Before he was elected mayor in 1969, Charles Stenvig was a burglary detective, best known in city politics for his active and noisy role in the police union. In 1969 Stenvig staged a surprising victory over the more experienced and better known Republican opponent, Dan Cohen. Running as an independent, Stenvig was an appealing candidate to those disenchanted with the Democratic social liberalism of the 1960s. Portraying himself as a tough, law-and-order type, he conveyed the image of a man who could stand up to the tumult and upheaval of the times.

Described by one former mayor as a man who views city affairs "from the perspective of a police superintendent,"[35] Charles Stenvig did not maintain a good working relationship with the city council. He was affiliated with neither political party and functioned as a lone ranger in city hall.

Former City Council President Louis DeMars characterized Stenvig as a "negative leader;" rather than trying to find a solution to a problem, he "kind of waited for someone else to do it and then he either signed it or vetoed it." Added DeMars, "Stenvig was afraid to vote his convictions; instead he voted the populace vote."[36]

In 1973 there seemed to be little doubt that the majority of the Minneapolis populace was against the building of the stadium. Of 600 people polled in a Minneapolis *Star* "Metropoll" in February of 1972, 62 percent of the Minneapolis residents were against the stadium, and only 31 percent favored it.[37] A similar poll conducted in December of 1972 found that Twin Cities residents were against the stadium's construction by a two-to-one margin.[38] Citizens were most adamant in their opposition to the stadium during the series of public hearings conducted in 1972. The residents objected to the project because they feared it would lead to traffic congestion, parking problems, increased pollution, and eventual taxpayer burden.

During the first few years of the stadium deliberations Mayor Stenvig made positive public statements about the project. But by the fall of 1972 his support for the stadium had softened. With his third election coming up in another year, the mayor wanted to absolve himself of any responsibility for the unpopular project. He asked that the issue be put to a citizens' referendum. But according to the City Charter, advisory referenda could not go on the ballot. To change the charter would require the approval of all 13 aldermen, but the aldermen would never adopt the proposal.

"The whole theory of representative government," said Council President Richard Erdall, "is that elected officials study issues and make educated decisions. Complicated questions require a great deal of study and understanding before a person votes and, generally speaking, you can't get that kind of study by the electorate." Erdall maintained that referenda afford elected officials with an opportunity to "abdicate their responsibilities."[39]

As far as elective politicking goes, however, this notion of "abdicating responsibilities" — of "deferring to public opinion" — can be a fruitful and politically savvy strategy. Charlie Stenvig's political shoes squeaked with ambivalence. The building of the stadium was personally attractive — he felt it would be an asset to the city. But a majority of his constituents did not share his positive feelings about the project. An election was coming up in less than a year. The last thing the mayor wanted to do was to associate himself with an unpopular project. The City Council voted in favor of the stadium by a ten to three margin. The City Charter specified that only nine votes were needed to override a mayor's veto. Stenvig was aware that a veto would meet with a Council override. But a veto was the mayor's gateway to the best of two worlds. If the stadium were a success, the mayor's actions would have no negative impact on his electoral position. If it turned into a financial disaster he could shove the blame onto the City Council.

Those involved with the issue in the early 70's say that this was exactly what Charles Stenvig was thinking. On February 6 the Mayor vetoed the stadium proposal. On February 7 the Council overrode his veto. According to Louis DeMars, Stenvig even told some people not to worry about the project, saying, "I may have to vote against it, but it will get passed."[40]

"Ironically Mayor Stenvig wanted the stadium as badly as anyone else," remembers David Roe. "He knew when he vetoed it that it would be overridden. He sat in the good position of opposing it and still getting it. The people who wanted the stadium would be happy. The people who didn't want it would say, 'at least you tried Mr. Mayor.' "[41]

But in March of 1973 Charles Stenvig could no longer straddle the issue; he could no longer achieve one objective while attempting to take the credit for another. Due to a completely unexpected circumstance, Stenvig was forced to make a choice. And this time it was a real choice.

## Government in Minneapolis

Like the chief executive in every city, the Minneapolis mayor is constantly required to "make choices." But often his decisions are insignificant. In Minneapolis the mayor lacks the formal power that is needed to make real legislative and administrative changes.

The structure of the city's government is determined by a 1920 city charter which provides for a weak mayor, strong council system. In Minneapolis the mayor has relatively little power when compared with his counterpart in other cities, such as Detroit, where the mayor is given greater formal powers. The Minneapolis mayor is elected for only a two-year term; in Detroit the mayor is elected for a four-year term. Only nine of the 13 aldermens' votes are required to override the mayor's veto in Minneapolis; in cities with stronger mayors, sometimes higher percentages on the council are needed to override. The Minneapolis mayor appoints the chief of police and a majority of the members of the city's commissions, but only with the council's consent. The council appoints the city attorney, the city engineer, the city clerk, and the city assessor. Legally the city council, with its combination of legislative and administrative powers, overshadows the Minneapolis mayor.[42]

City elections formerly were non-partisan — the ballots and voting machines were not allowed to show any party affiliation for the different candidates. Such a system made it relatively easy for an independent, with the support of neither the Democratic or Republican party, to get elected.

The "weak mayor," city government structure makes it almost impossible for the city to be governed by any kind of political machine or party boss. But the system also causes power to be extremely dispersed. Thus the relationship between the mayor and the council is often tense. It is difficult for the mayor to be a leader when he is only elected for two-year terms and given little formal authority while in office. In a study of Minneapolis politics, Alan Altshuler gives the following description of one Minneapolis mayor, P. Kenneth Peterson:

> (The Mayor) does not actively sponsor anything. He waits for private groups to agree on a project. If he likes it, he endorses it. Since he has no formal power with which to pressure the council himself, he feels that the private groups must take the responsibility for getting their plan accepted. He never attempts to coerce aldermen. Instead he calls them into his office to reason with them.[43]

This lack of formal power does not preclude the emergence of strong mayors, however. Hubert Humphrey would be characterized as a "leader" mayor, a mayor who wielded a great deal of influence. In fact Humphrey once said that being mayor of Minneapolis was the best job that he ever had. But Humphrey's influence was based on informal, charismatic power rather than legal, tangible authority. Remarks former Mayor Arthur Naftalin, "Because of the structure of government in Minneapolis, there is a built-in tension between the mayor and the council. The mayor is held accountable by the voters for city government actions but he often can do little to affect them." He adds, "People get mad at the mayor because the council decides to put a one-way street in front of their houses. They don't understand that the one-way street wasn't initiated by the mayor."[44]

The strong-council, weak-mayor system is frustrating to a mayor who wants to play a strong leadership role. It also can be politically damaging when the mayor is held accountable for unpopular policies over which he or she has little if any control. Yet this blurring of responsibilities is not always undesirable; it

23

gives the mayor an opportunity to dawdle, to tiptoe around hotly contested issues. But even under a "weak mayor" system the city's chief executive is sometimes called upon to make a consequential decision. For however slight his or her formal powers might be, situations arise which allow the mayor to exercise authority, or, as was the case with Charles Stenvig, force him to exercise that authority.

## The Plot that Failed

One of the most intoxicating ingredients of American politics is that its sagas so often hinge upon the smallest quirks and the unexpected coincidences. Perhaps Americans view politics in this way because their country's history has been so brief. Some claim that the country's preoccupation with media coverage fosters a sensationalist attitude towards political happenings. Whatever the reasoning, the evidence is clear. Would a governor named Jerry Brown have ever guessed that an insect as small as a medfly would throw his constituency into a state of political turmoil? In January of 1976, would the American public have believed that some well-placed appearances in Iowa, made by a peanut farmer from Georgia, would launch the campaign of the next president of the United States? And five years earlier, would another U.S. President have fathomed that a man named G. Gordon Liddy would one day strike the match that obliterated his political career?

Sometimes the unexpected occurs at the right time and at the right place; the sun glows on the lucky politician. Other times we find the opposite. Such was the plight of Mr. Albert Hum.

In February of 1973 Mr. Hum was one of the seven members of the Minneapolis Board of Estimates and Taxation, which had to approve the sale of the stadium's bonds. Five of the seven board members were required to vote in favor of the proposal in order for it to pass. Charles Stenvig served on the board and he was obligated to vote against the bond sale because of his earlier veto. Another board member, Donald G. Hanson, also said that he would vote against the proposal. But it looked as though the project would just barely clear its last barrier. The remaining five board members said that they were in favor of the stadium.

A few days before the vote a subplot developed. It was discovered that board member Hum, in the throes of a marital separation, no longer resided in the city of Minneapolis. Mr. Hum was temporarily housed in suburban Golden Valley. Found to be in violation of the city charter's residency requirement, Hum hastily submitted his resignation.

The mayor was obligated to appoint a new board member. No longer could he straddle the issue by publicly denouncing the project while privately voicing his approval. He was driven to make a choice. He could appoint someone to the board who would insure the stadium's passage; or he could choose someone who would kill it. Because of his earlier veto and public condemnations of the project, Charles Stenvig had little room to maneuver. He was, in the words of one stadium proponent, "pretty well locked in."[45]

There was a catch, however. The council, aligned in favor of the stadium, had to approve Stenvig's appointment. On February 21, the Mayor nominated Norman Selby, a former chairman of the far-right Minnesota T-party, to replace Hum. The Council turned down Selby's nomination, along with Stenvig's five following nominees. All of the nominees were staunch conservatives, firmly against large public expenditures. They were either opposed to the stadium or refused to say how they would vote on the issue.

On March 31 Stenvig paid a surprise visit to a city council meeting. He informed the aldermen that he would block stadium approval by refusing to appoint a new board member. Stenvig also announced that he would not vote on the stadium until Minneapolis residents had the opportunity to vote on the project in a referendum. "The Mayor is more concerned with himself and his own future electability than the future of the city," declared one angry alderman, "Mayor Weathervane has acted again. When it gets down to the critical moment," the alderman noted, "Charlie lacks the backbone to carry the ball over the goal line."[46]

Two months later petitioners gathered the 15,000 signatures

needed to force a vote on whether the city should hold referenda on all projects which cost more than $15 million. In June the amendment passed. Voters' approval was required on all major projects before the Board of Estimates could borrow money to finance them. Unless public opinion radically changed in Minneapolis, it was now literally impossible for the stadium's proponents to get the proposal passed in the city.

The stadium's rollercoaster journey through the workings of city government had come to an abrupt halt. Temporarily the engine choked, but the stadium's advocates were not ready to bury it. The stakes, in fact, were getting higher.

For 20 years Metropolitan Stadium was the capital of tailgating culture in America.

Mike Lynn

Max Winter

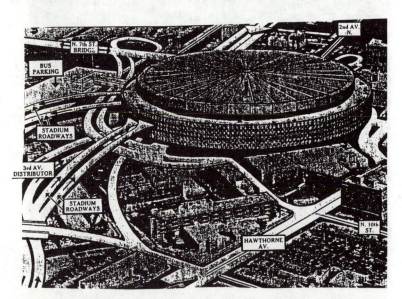

The first scheme for a downtown Minneapolis domed stadium was a "doughnut," an arena surrounded by a parking ramp.

"The Minnesota Vikings are not a Minnesota team. They're a company that plays football and happens to be located in Minnesota. They're here to make money. They're not here because they love us . . . no matter how much we love them." — Former State Sen. Steve Keefe.

# 2

# A GOVERNMENT RESPONDS

The evolution of the Minnesota stadium is a virtual clinic in the view it gives us of the anatomy of a public project which flows from a private interest. The story illustrates how a project becomes a matter of government concern, why it is defined as being one which serves the public interest, and how it consequently evolves onto the government's agenda.

Why did government get involved in the sports stadium business? How did it respond? How did government's formal structure and established political values affect its actions?

Begin with the Minneapolis Council. To understand why it got involved in the stadium project, which in effect was a subsidy to a private industry — the Vikings — is to recognize the uniqueness of that industry. The Minneapolis city government reacted to the stadium differently from how it reacted to other public projects. Debates over issues like the building of the government center or the airport were not embroiled in the politics of public subsidy. Their construction was not viewed as a selected benefit to a private industry. The stadium's issue context, on the other hand, depended on the workings of the professional sports industry, the economics of stadium construction, the relationship between the public and the sports industry, and the value of the stadium to the community.

## The Industry: Professional Sports

For many years there was an idyllic image of organized football and baseball as sports. They were good clean fun which inspired youngsters to take to the sandlots instead of the street corners, national pastimes which could make only positive contributions to our society. That portrait went largely unchallenged in this country. "In many respects professional baseball typifies the basic ideals of the American people," concluded a 1952 Congressional Report, "Fairness and clean competition are the passwords of the sport."[1]

In 1922 the Supreme Court ruled that professional baseball was not within interstate commerce and hence was not subject to antitrust laws. This ruling set the precedent for the legal exemptions afforded to other major league sports. Before the 1950's Congress never questioned this special status awarded to the sports industry. Since that time nearly 300 pieces of legislation concerning professional sports have been introduced in Congress.[2] Antitrust suits, player strikes, franchise relocations, and contested broadcast monopolies have induced the public and their elected representatives to take a second look at the sports industry. Although there remain vestiges of a reverence for sports in this country today, the myth has given way to a more pragmatic view: pro sports is a business. "It's a sport," said Howard Cosell, "to the fans only."[3]

In his study of professional sports, Henry Demmert defines the industry as "firms or clubs which field teams of major league quality (baseball, football, basketball and hockey) which are bound by a series of formal interfirm agreements dealing with the economic, sporting and other aspects of that relationship."[4] The revenue for each club is derived from the sale of tickets, broadcast rights, players contracts, and in some cases concessions and stadium rental. Although team owners are not required to divulge financial data (with the exception of a small number of publicly owned teams) there is no doubt that owning a sports team can be a lucrative and stable investment. The magnitude of the profits is contingent on the sport, however. Professional soccer, as a newcomer to the American sports industry, presents a risky venture. And a pro football club — which is reported to make between $20 and $25 million in annual revenues, with $14 million of that sum coming from television contracts — takes in much greater profits than most pro baseball teams.[5] Yet even in baseball and soccer the tax loopholes and potential big league profits make an investment into one of the established sports leagues valuable. "It's awfully hard to make money in this game," lamented Joseph Inglehart, former owner of the Baltimore Orioles, "But I've never heard of anybody losing any either."[6]

What does a sports club produce? As an employer of athletic talent, it produces entertainment in the form of games. But unlike conventional businesses, its product can only be produced in simultaneous cooperation with another firm. In other words, the sports firms are interdependent; they need each other to make profits. This is why they join into leagues which make collective decisions, essentially creating a cartel. Professional sports is in fact the OPEC of American businesses. While each firm is an independent profit-maximizer, all of the firms together, represented by a league, make decisions which restrict competition, thereby increasing the profits of the individual members. Each club has "territorial rights to a given market."[7] It is thus isolated from direct price competition with other league members. Unless the league allows a city to have two teams, a team cannot locate in an area which already has a team. Established clubs control the addition of new ones by requiring multi-million dollar fees to join the league and by holding absolute power over franchise expansion.

Such collusive activities would not be allowed in any other American enterprise subject to the regulation of antitrust laws. When there is a high demand for a product in almost every other industry, new firms are induced to compete, eventually lowering the cost of the product to the consumer. But given the protected nature of the professional sports industry and the strength of the established cartels, those rebel leagues which attempt to compete outside of the cartels (e.g., the now extinct World Football League) lack the capital and clout to survive. "Many more cities could support teams if the supply wasn't limited," says Professor Roger Noll. "In recent years, as sports have become more popular, the response of the monopolist has been predictable — ticket prices go up and up . . . the monopolist simply takes in higher revenues." According to Noll, team owners "dole franchises out just as any other monopolist would, creating a contrived scarcity."[8]

It is this "contrived scarcity" — this undersupply and excess demand — which serves as a backdrop to the contested issue of public subsidies for stadiums. To put it another way, there are more cities that want teams than there are teams for cities. Government leaders who either want to gain popularity by acquiring a franchise or are afraid of losing public support because a team abandons their community, will make extremely accommodating financial offers, in the form of stadium subsidies, to coax million-dollar sports organizations to either remain in or move to their areas. These officials are not necessarily naive or ill-intentioned. Often times they are simply responding to public demand. "If the people in this community want a team badly enough," the wisdom goes, "then they damn well better build a stadium." The teams' owners aren't going to do it.[9] "Build your own stadium?" Edward Bennett Williams, Washington Redskins president, once exclaimed, "We could never do that. The economics of stadium operation are impossible unless you have an assurance of subsidies from the city or state governments.[10]

One can certainly sympathize with the irate Minneapolis City Council member who declared "if the jocks want a stadium, then the jocks can pay for it."[11] But given the nature of the professional sports industry — the fact that there is a scarcity of teams and that in the early seventies many cities were willing to build glamorous sports arenas in order to retain those teams — it is understandable that the city council wanted to build one of its own. Ten years later the council might not have been as eager to sponsor such a frivolous project, but in 1971 Minneapolis was just beginning to establish a reputation as a thriving, sophisticated metropolitan area. Council members thought that a stadium would gild that image. The economics of stadium construction might have been tough. But the thought of remaining a stadium-less city, and what would be much worse, a minor-league city, was tougher.

## The Good: Stadiums

"If you are going to build a major sports stadium today, you start by digging a hole. That is where you are going to to build the stadium. And that is probably where the stadium is going to put you."[12]

Ancient Rome used to tax its brothels to support its coliseum. American cities today lack such a convenient taxable institution which can shoulder the costs of sports arenas. Here the most common way of financing a stadium is to have the public pay for it. While a handful of them are privately financed, about 70 percent of U.S. stadiums are owned and operated by the government.[13] In some communities it is the city that owns the arena, in others it is the county or state. Some stadiums are owned jointly by several levels of government.

The public's investment in stadiums has not been a profitable one. Very few stadiums break even and many of them incur large deficits every year. In his study of the subsidies of stadiums and arenas, economist Benjamin Okner identified two ways in which local governments that own sports facilities subsidize professional sports teams: directly, by pricing stadium rents below the economic value of the facilities, and indirectly, by foregoing taxes on the stadiums.[14]

Even stadiums which are privately financed have been built on tax-exempt property. While privately financed stadiums do not come with the Pandora's box of problems associated with publicly financed stadiums, they have presented some difficulties of their own. After an unsuccessful effort by some Boston civic leaders to build a football stadium in their city, Boston entrepreneur Phil David Fine decided to finance the stadium. He built one for only $7.5 million, but the stadium, a bare-bone building of few amenities, stands 26 miles outside of the city. The half-domed Texas stadium in Dallas was built by Cowboys' owner Clint Murchison. In addition to moving the team from the South Dallas Cotton Bowl to suburban Irving, Murchison required that each season ticket-holder buy a 35-year bond to help finance the stadium. Dodger Stadium in Los Angeles was privately financed by owner Walter O'Malley in 1962. O'Malley decided to save money by not installing drinking fountains. In the wake of the public outcry that followed, O'Malley was reported to snort: "Let them drink beer."[15] Los Angeles health officials later ordered that fountains be installed.

But the problems encountered by the residents of communities which house privately-owned stadiums pale beside those of taxpayers who have paid for the stadiums themselves. Stadium advocates generally understate the probable costs of stadium construction in order to drum up public support. The Louisiana Superdome, for instance, started out as a $35 million project and grew to approximately $163 million. Although part of the project was privately funded, a four percent hotel-motel tax instituted to pay the debt service could not meet the $10.3 million annual debt service fee. In 1976 *Business Week* reported that property taxpayers would have to pick up at least $5 million of the Superdome's debt service cost each year.[16]

Those stadiums which do make money, in many cases the two-team stadiums, do well enough to pay their expenses but are unable to meet the interest and principal on their bond issues. The most common way of financing stadiums is with revenue bonds which are backed by the arena's income. But when the stadium doesn't make enough money the revenue bonds become general obligation bonds for which property taxpayers are responsible. These "hybrid bonds" do not require the public commitment demanded of bonds originally issued as general obligation. New Orleans Mayor Moon Landrieu described the Superdome's bond issue: "It walks and talks like full faith and credit, but it's not."[17]

Cities derive most of their revenue from property taxes. If local taxes are not raised to finance stadium subsidies, then, writes

Benjamin Okner, "the real cost of the subsidy to the city involves the reduction of expenditures that otherwise would have been made with these funds (such as expenditures on education, health, police, and fire prevention)." Okner concludes, "to the extent that subsidized rentals are not passed on to consumers in the form of lower prices or to the players in the form of higher salaries, the prime beneficiaries of the local government subsidies are the owners of the sports teams."[18]

In light of the tremendous cost overruns and taxpayer burdens incurred by the public in other cities, it is understandable that the Minneapolis city council searched for a "safeguarded" method of stadium finance. To its credit, it demanded that the business community pledge to pay part of any deficit that might result. But in view of the large deficits incurred by other stadiums, the $600,000 annual business guarantee might not have been enough. The burden consequently would have fallen on the special tax assessment district, composed of local business-es, both big and small. Had the yearly deficit been extremely large, corporate wails would have undoubtedly rent the northern skies. If the experience of taxpayers elsewhere was an augury, the burden eventually would have fallen on the public, either directly by means of a special tax, or indirectly in the form of a lower level of public services or a higher cost of business goods.

## The Market: Its Winners and Losers

In 1978 Los Angeles Rams' owner Carroll Rosenbloom decided to move his team to Anaheim Stadium, 30 miles away from the Los Angeles Coliseum where the Rams had been playing for 33 years. The Rams owner was drawn to the Anaheim Stadium in part because the offer included an option to buy 95 acres of adjoining parking lot — now valued at $33 million — for $7.6 million. "The bottom line," says James F. Hardy, general manager of the Los Angeles Coliseum, "was that Rosenbloom didn't move a football franchise; he made a real estate deal.[19]

When it comes to striking deals between the cities which build the stadiums and the sports industry which uses them, the industry is blessed with all of the negotiating advantages. In fact it has the opportunity to profit from the city's losses. And that's the bottom line.

"In rent negotiations," notes Okner, "the team is in a bargaining position superior to that of the city."[20] Since the city cannot move the stadium, it is left with few choices: it can rent the stadium to the team, it can let the stadium sit unused, or it can tear it down. The team, on the other hand, is faced with more attractive alternatives: it can play in the city's stadium, it can play in another stadium in the same city, or it can move the team to another city.[21]

Los Angeles is hardly the first city to lose a team to the suburbs. New York, Detroit, Dallas and Boston have all had similar experiences. Yet however far these teams have chosen to wander from their original host, they have still managed to retain the city's name. In the case of the New York Giants, who are now playing in Hackensack, N.J., the city itself — at least in name — has transcended state boundaries.

Several years ago when George Halas, owner of the Chicago Bears, was looking for a new home for his team, there was talk of playing in suburban Arlington Heights. The news provoked Richard Daley, then mayor of Chicago, to give an acid-laced lecture on geography. If Halas was going to move his team to Arlington Heights, Daley said, then he had better call them the Arlington Heights Bears.[22]

Yet the city, or for that matter, the state, has no patent on its name. All's fair in the psychodelia of pro sports. At least cities which lose their teams to the suburbs are still able to retain the team as a "standard-bearer" and most resident fans remain a negotiable distance from the games. Other cities have not been so lucky.

After Minneapolis businessman Robert Short paid almost $10 million to buy the Washington Senators he shocked the nation's capital by moving the baseball team to Texas. The operators of Robert F. Kennedy Memorial Stadium tried to entice the team back with accommodative rental agreements. But Short had a better deal in Texas. "Sports-page identification helps my trucking business so much," said Short, "that the team will be worth the price if it just manages to break even."[23]

While the Washington Senators had not been playing to a full house, for twelve years the Oakland Raiders football team had generated 53,500-seat sellouts in the Oakland arena.[24] But the Raiders' owner Al Davis got a better deal from Los Angeles. Oakland's promise of $9 million in improvements was outrun by the $19 million Los Angeles package which included ninety-nine luxury boxes added to the stadium the Rams had vacated when they moved to Anaheim.[25] The N.F.L. refused the Raiders' move by a vote of 20-0. Three-fourths of the teams are required to approve the move. Yet despite the league's disapproval and the city of Oakland's lawsuit against the team's owner, Al Davis still moved the team. He did it with the court's permission — a Los Angeles court to be sure.

Sports owners are able to manipulate franchise locations and wheedle lucrative stadium deals out of cities because the political market in which the cities and team negotiate their deals is an imbalanced one. The "winners" (the owners) who stand to benefit from a team's locality change are highly concentrated. They have a vast stake in the issue, usually running to millions of dollars. The "losers" — the fans in an area which will be left high and dry with an empty stadium, or the public who will be forced to contribute to the cost of a new stadium — are greatly dispersed. Although their combined loss may be larger than the owner's gain, each individual suffers relatively little when compared with the owner's potential benefit. In a political market such as this one, it is difficult for the "losers" to organize in order to rally against the highly concentrated and well-financed "winners." This imbalanced political market, along with the previously mentioned "contrived scarcity" of teams, allows sports teams to profit at the cities' expense.

Members of the Minneapolis City Council were aware of the risk in financing a sports stadium. They realized that the project was an unpopular one — that in spite of the business guarantee, their constituents were afraid of being skewered with the bill. If the stadium was a disaster, it would most likely hurt incumbent aldermen at the polls. If it were a success, it wouldn't necessarily inspire voters to re-elect the council member. So whatever stirred these elected officials to want to build a stadium in the first place?

## Government Involvement: Justifications

A public good has been defined as "any good such that if one person in a group consumes it, it cannot feasibly be withheld from the others in the group."[26] Although a stadium wouldn't be considered a public good in the purest sense (its use is not available to all, since only selected people can afford tickets), it is a kind of public good. As far as the stadium serves to attract or hold a sports team, it can be viewed as a public good. No one who lives in the city or state is excluded from claiming possession of the ball club — whether they are "our Vikings," or "our Muskrats." Nor are the vast majority of residents excluded from watching the team on television or listening to a game on the radio. The stadium itself is a public good if it houses events which are free to the public or events for which ticket prices are not prohibitive.

So the stadium is a quasi-public good; a public good which selectively benefits the owners and employees of the teams who use the stadium and the ticket-holders who can afford to buy seats for the more expensive events. The stadium may also selectively benefit surrounding businesses. But it is not the selective benefits which elected officials emphasize when they assert that a stadium will be a positive addition to a community. It is the general benefits — the "public interest" justifications — that they run up the flagpole. While the claims of stadium proponents are often exaggerated and for the most part impossible to verify, the intent here is to simply present the justifications given for government involvement.[27]

### Tangible Benefits

Stadium advocates usually focus on the tangible benefits that the stadium will bring to a city: The stadium will be an economic asset. It will enlarge the tax base. It will infuse the community with jobs. When Minneapolis City Coordinator Tommy Thompson contended that the stadium would "spur $200 million in nearby development and bring in an increase of $5 to 6 million annually in downtown business,"[28] he was talking about the tangible, economic benefits that he felt the stadium would bring to the city. Often stadium promoters overinflate the potential benefits of a stadium. But there is evidence that after a stadium has been built, both surrounding businesses and state and local governments come to depend on it for "game day" revenue. The baseball strike during the summer of 1981 injured the economies of cities accustomed to big attendance at ballgames. Every cancelled Yankees game was said to cost the New York City Parks Department about $7,000 and the city's subway system about $6,000. In Philadelphia officials estimated that the city lost at least $78,700 in tax revenue on each unplayed game.[29]

Increased tax revenue was one of the economic justifications given for the government's involvement in the Minneapolis stadium project. It was argued that the stadium would bring visitors to the city who would spend money in the restaurants, the bars, the hotels, and the stores, thereby enlarging the city's tax base. The stadium was also commended as a project which would bring jobs into the area. As Minnesota labor leader David Roe, one of the most tenacious and vocal stadium advocates, maintained: "If it's good for the community, whether it be the building of the stadium or the expansion of the hotel industry, if it will help the area grow . . . it has to be good for us."[30]

*Intangible Benefits*

When business leader Harvey MacKay declared that without the Vikings and the Twins, "the Twin Cities would be well on the way to becoming a frozen Omaha,"[31] he was describing in part the intangible benefits that the teams bring to the area. A stadium is heralded for the spirit and sense of pride it will instill in a city. The publicity a team generates for the area is said to enhance the community, not only economically, but also psychologically and spiritually. A stadium becomes a symbol that the city is willing to undertake ambitious projects. Hosting major league sports gives the city "big league" status. The teams which play in the stadium serve as the city's banner carriers, something like the knights were to Camelot.

"Professional sports teams make immeasurable contributions to the good will and spirit of a community," said a New York state legislator when he introduced a $350 million stadium bill in 1973, "and without this elusive thing called spirit no economic well being can infuse a community with enthusiasm and a sense of purpose."[32] Simply because it is impossible to quantify the intangible benefits which a stadium may generate does not make them any less potent as both an emotional rallying cry and a valid justification for stadium advocates. Even if a person finds the game of professional football revolting or thinks of the pleasure derived from an afternoon of baseball-watching as infantile, he or she must acknowledge that professional sports provides additional entertainment opportunities for community residents.

"I'm not an avid baseball fan," says Harvey MacKay, "but I do know that having the Twins helps out the community." MacKay likens the teams to the Guthrie Theater and Orchestra Hall. "Even if you live a block away from the Guthrie and you never see a play," he says, "it doesn't matter . . . you'll still benefit. Take those assets away and you have a backward community. That's why we worked so hard for the stadium."[33]

## The Way It Works in Minneapolis

The justifications voiced by the Minneapolis promoters in the stadium debates were identical to the arguments entered in other communities. Like civic leaders in many cities, the majority of the Minneapolis government officials were convinced that the construction of a multi-million dollar stadium would serve the public interest. But despite similar "public interest" justifications, city governments have responded differently in planning and financing their stadiums.

Some cities, such as Seattle and Detroit, have experienced long, incendiary battles over the financing and location of their stadiums. In a few localities, (e.g. Boston and Dallas), the stadium was financed without a penny of taxpayers' money and planned with a minimum of public input. In some places the proposal was placed on a citizens' ballot; in other cities, such as Minneapolis, it was not. In Denver a stadium proposal was put to a referendum and the result was no new stadium whatsoever. New Orlean's Superdome and New York's renovation of Yankee Stadium have incurred enormous cost overruns, while the Pontiac Silverdome and the Foxboro stadium have not.

While these varied performances can be accounted for in part by the type of stadium (luxurious vs. skeletal), the state of the economy at the time of the stadium's construction, and the city's economic base, they are also determined by the city's political system. Stadiums are in this sense only barometers measuring the way a community's government confronts a political struggle. "In some cities, decisions generally turn on the struggle of politicians, parties, and interest groups for some advantage," write Edward Banfield and James Q. Wilson in *City Politics*. "In other cities, politics seems to be entirely absent: there are no conflicts and no struggle for power; matters are decided, at least seemingly, on purely technical grounds."[34]

The way in which a city confronts any project — whether it be a stadium or a zoo — depends on its political system. This includes the urban government's formal structure and voting procedures. It also includes its informal arrangements — its relationship with organized interests and the community's political culture.

The Minneapolis government is characterized as a "strong council-weak mayor" urban government. Until recently, elections were non-partisan and the mayor and the council members are only elected for two-year terms. Thus power is not highly concentrated in one person. Other cities such as New York have "strong mayor" systems, where the mayor shares power with the council but is granted vaster formal authority to appoint administrative heads and influence budget decisions. The mayor is considered to be the leader of the Council. In the evolution of several stadium projects, the most notable being the renovation of Yankee Stadium and the active role played by Mayor Lindsay, the mayor has been the catalyst for the project's approval.

Yet even in "strong mayor" arrangements power is dispersed

among the many independent boards and special districts which have been created to share in the administration of city government.[35] In New York, for instance, a proliferation of special boards and districts exercise authority, including a Board of Estimates. If it were not for the required approval of the Board of Estimates in Minneapolis, a stadium would most likely have been built in 1973. The dispersal of power — the authority delegated above and beyond the council-mayor structure — served to defeat the proposal.

Dispersed power and the resulting multiplicity of decision-making points, where a project's passage can be slowed and sometimes irreversibly halted, is one of the defining characteristics of the American political system. Found at local, state and national levels, this separation of powers is intended to prohibit one political actor or one group of actors from wielding excessive power. But to be effective, to move policies and projects through its operational maze, a city's decision-making authority must be firmly lodged in some part of the government's structure, whether it be in the mayor, in an appointed board, or in a citizens' referendum.

Some cities have tried to reduce the political struggling which results from dispersed power by adopting a council-manager form of government. The thrust behind the council-manager system is to take the "politics" out of decision-making; to run government as a business. Yet the political decisions are still made. Buildings are erected, neighborhoods are divided, but there is less public political clashing than there would be in a mayor-council system. In some cases a strong council manager emerges, a person who is indirectly accountable to the people through the elected council, but not directly tied to the voting public. In other places, like Dallas, the council is dominated by a strong and well-organized business community.

His independent status undoubtedly helped Stenvig in his quest for office. And if a certified Democrat or Republican had been mayor there would have been a much greater chance that he or she would have voted for the stadium. Depending on his or her position with the party and the electorate, a mayor belonging to a major party may have felt pressure from the party to vote in favor of the stadium proposal, both as mayor and as member of the Board of Estimates.

## Who Runs the Town?

Differences in legal powers however, don't fully explain why the urban governments would react differently to an identical project. Cities differ in the extent and kind of influence exercised by the business community. In many cities, business and government are instinctively clashing on every issue from the enactment of zoning laws to the indexing of taxes. In other places business interests dominate government. A few cities — such as Minneapolis — are known for the cooperative relationship which has developed between business and government. Although their interests collide on many issues, on those where they find common ground — a stage of mutual accommodation — the public and private sectors can work together to reach solutions beneficial to both.

This "business tradition" stems in part from the expectations placed upon the business community; the tradition that newspaper owner John Cowles Jr. referred to when he talked about the "pattern" which had developed over the years. A community also fosters a "government tradition" which partly determines what situations its leaders feel are appropriate for government action. A community's "political culture" has been defined as common expectations of government which are acquired by the people of the community.[36] People learn to expect who is powerful or who will play a certain role because they, or their predecessors, did it that way.

"Government is not considered to be an enemy of the private sector, instead it is an aid, a helper . . . there is a spirit here that government does not necessarily have to be onerous."[37] Former Mayor Naftalin's words capture the political culture in Minneapolis. The location and financing decisions for the Minneapolis stadium could never have been a completely private matter. This was true not only because a potential financer was unavailable, but also because local government action is traditionally a vital force in the city.

Contrast this political culture with the one prevailing in Dallas. The business power in Dallas is concentrated in the Dallas Citizens' Council, a highly visible group of downtown business-men and a dominant force in the decisions of the city council. In most American cities the business community wields a great deal of influence, but in Dallas it is particularly powerful. As John Bainbridge writes in *The Super Americans,* "One trait above all dominates the Dallas personality — reverence for business . . . it is a city of the businessmen, by the businessmen, and for the businessmen."[38] The Dallas government will often shun issues with which other urban governments automatically involve themselves. An example of this is the minimal public role in the re-location of the Dallas sports stadium.

The Dallas Cowboys had always played their games at the Cotton Bowl in South Dallas. But by the mid-sixties owner Clint Murchison refused to accept the stadium's outmoded facilities and the deteriorating conditions of the black slums which surrounded the arena. The Dallas city council recognized that the Cowboy's presence in the area was an asset for South Dallas. The games brought in much-needed revenue. Yet the council did little to fight Murchison's decision to move his team to Irving, Dallas' largest suburb.

The Cowboys' owner financed the stadium privately. Not a tax dollar was spent. Season tickets were tied in with the bond purchases. Stadium boxes cost $50,000 in 35-year bonds. Seats between the 30-yard lines required a $1,000 bond purchase. Most of the other seats went for $250 in bonds. Parking spaces were allocated according to the price of the seat. Of the 32,000 season ticket holders at the Cotton Bowl, where the Cowboys played through the 1970 season, 10,000 of them did not buy bonds at the new Texas stadium. "Yes I'd say we lost a whole group in the $12,000 to $20,000 salary range who couldn't afford to buy the bonds," Murchison told one reporter, "If we discriminated against them, we discriminated against them, but no more than all America discriminates against people who don't have enough money to buy everything they want.[39]

Minneapolis government officials obviously would have welcomed an offer from Max Winter to privately finance a new stadium. But if the Met had originally been located in Minneapolis and Winter tried to build a new stadium in Bloomington, the political brawl would have been fierce. No such fury arose in Dallas.

The Minneapolis political culture also dictated an active role for business in the stadium project. The pattern of business involvement made it improbable that a Minneapolis stadium would be built exclusively with public money. Although the 1971 stadium proposal was eventually defeated, it could have never come far without a business pledge to cover deficits. This was not the case in other cities.

During the 1960's the government of New York grew faster than any other industry in town. To provide for the high level of services demanded by its citizens, the city of New York pumps millions of dollars of federal, state and city funds into its economy each year. In many cases, this public funding is essential: the needs cannot be met through the private market. In other cases the public funding has led to inefficiences in services and bungling in their administration. In any case, New Yorkers are accustomed to government intervention.

When Mayor Lindsay announced in March of 1971 that New York City would acquire and renovate Yankee Stadium he said, ". . . the city regards modernization of the stadium and retention of the Yankees and the Giants as vital to the recreational, economic and cultural health of the city."[40] Faced with the city's high tax rates, Lindsay realized that the teams might well join other businesses which had abandoned New York for greener pastures. It had already been jilted by the baseball Giants and Dodgers. Lindsay wanted to save both the city and his administration from other defections. But there was little he could do when five months later the Giants signed a 30-year lease with the New Jersey Sports and Exposition Authority to occupy the new Meadowlands sports complex. Within four years Mayor Lindsay's original $24 million plan to keep the Yankees and the Giants ballooned into a baseball-only stadium, at a cost of $125 million to the taxpayers. In the lease with the Yankees the city promised to upgrade the neighborhood surrounding the stadium. There were plans for pedestrian malls, tree-lined streets and a running track. But by 1975, when the original estimate for the stadium rehabilitation had increased nearly five times what it had been in 1971, the city asked the Yankees' management to be released from that part of the lease.[41]

The stadium experiences in New York, Dallas, and Minneapolis dramatize how a particular kind of public good, with a particular mix of governmental and private interests, is defined and financed. The scope of the governments' involvement was determined by the nature of the stadium projects. The stadiums in turn were inextricably tied to the workings of the professional sports industry. They were in fact gambling chips used to bargain with that industry. The governments' responses — the different ways in which the arenas were battled-over and built — mirrors the historic and cultural differences in those cities with respect to the role of government. The financing and location of a football stadium is hardly a critical business of government. But it can illustrate how people *look* at government, and more importantly, how much they are willing to trust it.

Decisions should be viewed in the context in which they are made. This policy-making frame shapes the power relationships which color a project's final outcome. It determines how and when and where the government will decide to take action. But inside of the frame — this is where things become more colorful. Business and labor, Democrats and Republicans, urbanites and suburbanites; in the politics of public interest it is the kaleidoscope of interests which gives the picture form.

**Harvey MacKay**  **Charles Stenvig**  **David Roe**

---

The Mr. Bill Show at the state legislature

1-31-79
Minneapolis Star and Tribune

47

"If it were allowable, I'd wring that little (Bloomington) mayor's neck." — Viking general manager Mike Lynn, in an outburst of diplomacy.

# 3

# THE STADIUM: 1973-1977

## The State Hears a Threat

"The people expressed themselves on the stadium issue in the vote in June," said the new Minneapolis Mayor, Albert Hofstede. "They have said that they are against the project . . . There's probably no way to revive it now."[1] In January of 1974 Democrat Hofstede replaced Charles Stenvig as mayor of Minneapolis. In spite of Stenvig's careful political posturing the mayor lost his bid for a third term. Not only was he a man without a stadium, but as of January, 1974, he was a man without an office. The thrust of the June referendum, which Stenvig enthusiastically supported, was that the city could not use its credit to borrow money for projects costing over $15 million without the voters' approval. Although the referendum did not specifically mention the stadium, the overwhelming number of "yes" votes were attributed to the voters' hostility towards it.

There was little chance that the stadium would be resurrected in 1974, despite Stenvig's defeat. The 1973 national recession, the increasing costs of construction, and the unfavorable state of the bond market made city council members more wary of the project than they had been the year before. Even if the proposal were revived, Minneapolis residents would most likely have voted against the bond authorization needed to finance the project. The message from the Minneapolis Council was clear: if a stadium were to be built, someone else would have to build it.

In March of 1975 the State Senate's Metropolitan and Urban Affairs Committee began hearing bills on the stadium issue. While in many cities stadium proposals were either adopted or rejected at the local level, it was not surprising that in Minnesota the state legislature took responsibility for the project. "The state of Minnesota has never hesitated to become involved in large scale metropolitan projects," observed University of Minnesota Professor Arthur Naftalin. "There is a long tradition of state involvement in local affairs."[2]

The state has been a pervasive force in local public education, for instance. A 1971 tax bill stipulated that state funds rather than local property taxes were to be used to pay the costs of operating local school districts. Many of the functions performed by municipalities in other states — sewage, water systems, transportation and land use planning — are, in the Twin Cities area, the responsibility of the Metropolitan Council. Representing a seven-county area, including the cities of Minneapolis and St. Paul, the Metropolitan Council was created by a 1967 legislative bill. Its 17 members are appointed by the governor.

Once the stadium became a matter of state rather than local concern, the focus of the debate shifted. "When the stadium was debated in the city council the major question was whether or not the project would be good for the city . . . whether or not it would spur economic development," recalled former Senator Steve Keefe. "But when the stadium got into the legislature, the questions became more complicated. Who will benefit from a stadium? What part of the state should the financial support come from? Is it a metropolitan or a statewide asset?" "We were asking," Keefe remembered, "not only if there should be a stadium, but also where it should be located."[3]

That the teams might abandon the Twin Cities unless they had a new stadium was a subliminal premise of the city council deliberations. The council, after all, had originally entered the sports business as a procurer, recruiting major league sports franchises to enhance the city's image and further its development. But when the proposals reached the legislature, the teams' threats to leave Minnesota, particularly the Vikings', emerged as the cardinal issue. The Vikings' lease was due to expire in 1975. Although Max Winter agreed to renew the Metropolitan stadium lease for another year, the Vikings' owner clearly signalled that he would not consider signing a long-term lease for the 48,700-seat stadium. N.F.L. commissioner Pete Rozelle acknowledged that a new Vikings' stadium was "not mandatory as far as the league is concerned." "But," he added, "I think it's mandatory for the franchise itself — with the current situation something will have to be done."[4]

## The Envelope Entrepreneur and his Teammates

"Had the Vikings and Twins been signed for five or ten years," claimed businessman Harvey MacKay, "there would have been nothing to talk about." But since the teams were reluctant to sign long-term leases, there was always the possibility they would abruptly leave the Twin Cities area. "You have to remember that Minnesota has competitors for its sports teams just as it has competitors for its other businesses," MacKay declared. "They offer us better rent, lower taxes, more flexibility, and sometimes even non-union plants. They give us all kinds of incentives to move our plants and to move our people . . . It's the same story with the Vikings."[5]

But Harvey MacKay is one businessman who is not likely to desert Minnesota. The son of a St. Paul newspaperman, MacKay bought a near-bankrupt envelope firm in 1960 and built it into a young empire. His business tops $10 million in sales every year and produces about 500 kinds of envelopes. Harvey MacKay is proud of the company. He is not offended when people kid him about his line of work. MacKay offers a reasonable explanation of why an envelope-maker can become a millionaire: "The real beauty of the business is that you can only use an envelope once, then you've got to buy a new one." "This business," he insists, "has a lot of charisma."[6]

A lively man in his forties, MacKay invests his work and company with a breathless verve matched only by his boosterism for the Twin Cities. "This community is a contrast to Dallas," he says. "There I think you're judged by your earnings per share, your wealth, the size of your home. Here I think you're judged by your involvement in the community."[7]

MacKay's community involvement and avid interest in sports made him well-suited to head the chamber of commerce's stadium task force. In 1973 Harvey MacKay approached 28 St. Paul and Minneapolis civic leaders to ask them if they would join the committee. Expecting "only ten or fifteen to say yes," MacKay was overjoyed when all 28 people agreed to serve on the task force. Although the group included some labor and non-business leaders, it was heavily weighted with business executives — the task force included 16 company presidents and three board chairmen of Minnesota corporations. The committee's first assignment was to determine whether there was a need for a new stadium. Then it would consider potential stadium sites and make a stadium proposal to the state legislature.

While the majority of the Twin Cities business people favored the construction of a new stadium, there were also some prominent figures who opposed the project. Newspaper owner John Cowles Jr. characterized those who either opposed the stadium or were reluctant to play a role in its initiation as "people whose businesses were national in nature so that they were less concerned with local developmental issues." For instance, Bill Spoor, the head of Pillsbury, "by and large liked the way things were in Bloomington and saw no particular reason to change things." Nor did General Mills, Pillsbury's historic competition in the Twin Cities, play an active role in promoting the stadium. "Some of the executives there," Cowles said, "were more interested in baseball than they were in football and they liked Met stadium as a baseball stadium."[8]

Honeywell president Ed Spencer, on the other hand, "immediately understood and responded to the developmental reasons for locating the stadium downtown." Although Spencer did not serve on the task force, his interest in reviving inner cities convinced him that the stadium project was valuable. Cowles explained: "Putting the stadium downtown provides much greater opportunities for poor and old people, for blacks, for people without cars. The Bloomington stadium really discriminated in favor of the prosperous, white, car-owning middle class. You saw very few black faces among the popcorn, beer, and peanut vendors."[9]

While social concerns influenced the business leaders' active promotion of the stadium, they were motivated by a good deal more than humanitarianism. Harvey MacKay liked the idea because of the publicity big-time sports generates for the area — publicity MacKay believes makes the Twin Cities attractive to potential companies and business talent. MacKay disagrees with those who maintain "since we don't pay for the buildings that house MacKay Envelope or Pillsbury, we shouldn't do it for the Vikings." There are good reasons why the public and private sectors should subsidize sports arenas, he argues, and it might have come straight out of a Viking yearbook: "When I open up my plant at 6:30 in the morning there are not 50 million people watching me do it. The chamber of commerce is constantly advertising for people to locate their plants here. The advertising the Vikings generate is free."[10]

MacKay's efforts to reinforce that argument produced a survey that might have inspired a television sitcom. He commissioned a research firm to find out how many times the word "Minnesota" was mentioned on television during the Vikings' four appearances in the Super Bowl. "And do you know how many times they said the word 'Minnesota'?" he asked gleefully, "279 times! And it didn't cost us a penny"[11]

Understandably, some of the stadium critics questioned whether the motives of the downtown stadium boosters were so civic. Perhaps it was more than local pride that aroused entrepreneurs like MacKay and Cowles to take such an active role in the stadium campaign. Maybe they were in it for the bucks.

Others dismissed their "altruistic" behavior as publicity stunts. The stadium presented an opportunity for business hotshots to build their egos and dramatize their civic consciousness. One stadium opponent likened the businessmen's tenacious civic chauvinism to the "behavior of adolescent boys." It was kind of a "macho trip," he said, "They became so caught up in the issue that they just lost perspective."[12]

Nobody could pinpoint the motivations behind every business-man who participated in the drive to build a stadium. Most likely several factors were at work: a desire to build the community; a fear the teams might vacate the area; the potential for direct or indirect profit; a bit of altruism; egotism. Whatever their motivations, their involvement was very visible, their preferences undisguised.

Harvey MacKay attacked the project with characteristic ebullience. He left his business for a year and devoted most of his undrainable energies to the stadium, twisting arms, peddling his optimism, and traveling the country to look at other stadiums. His task force hired Real Estate Research Corporation of Chicago to conduct a feasibility study to determine whether a new or renovated stadium made sense. The $25,000 cost was shared by the Twin Cities' chambers of commerce. Minneapolis picked up 60 percent of the tab, St. Paul the rest.

The resulting 38-page study estimated the costs of several options. Doming and remodeling the Met would cost from $49 million to $54 million. Doming and enlarging the University of Minnesota's Memorial stadium would cost between $38.5 and $40.2 million. A football stadium without a dome might cost anywhere from $28 to $90 million, a domed football stadium from $39 to $115 million, and a multi-purpose domed stadium from $50 to $126 million.[13]

If the wide-ranging figures presented by the feasibility study were vague, the task force's recommendations were more so. They suggested a domed multi-purpose stadium, but they declined to specify how the stadium should be financed or where it should be located.

Feasibility researchers usually read the political winds. Financing and locating the stadium were delicate questions better left to the politicians. And in the fall of 1974 civic leaders of a

Minneapolis suburb called Bloomington were more than pleased to provide state legislators with some earnest advice about where the stadium should be built.

## Bloomington Takes the Ball

Although Bloomington's stadium study group lacked the funds, notoriety, and organizational advantages of its downtown counterparts, it was blessed with an invaluable resource, something the cities could only dream of having.

Bloomington had the Minnesota Twins and Vikings.

And Bloomington civic leaders were convinced that either an additional 7,000 seats at the Met or an open-air football stadium adjacent to it would keep them there. While the Bloomington corps could not afford a $25,000 feasibility study to make their case, they were not going to be outtalked or outmuscled in their attempts to prod state legislators to make the "right" decision on the stadium issue. Like the downtown people, the Bloomington task force took advantage of their assets.

In the fall of 1974, Bloomington officials invited the state's most eminent decision-makers and their spouses to an elaborate "Vikings' Weekend." The list of invited guests reportedly topped 500. The weekend included cocktail parties, dinner, free accomodations in a Bloomington hotel, a tailgate party, tickets to the Bears-Vikings game, and an impassioned pitch for a Bloomington stadium. While most of the expenses for the football extravaganza were paid by the city's "hospitality industry" (a group of Bloomington hotels, bars, and restaurants), the suburb's city council allocated $3,000 of public money to help pay the costs.

For state legislators accustomed to receiving invites to "bean feeds" and county fairs, this was surely an unprecedented gala. Bloomington's generosity did evoke anger from some of the invited guests, however. Senator Nick Coleman, the Senate Majority Leader, declared that he was "appalled" by the invitation. The St. Paul Democrat called the spectacle "the kind of heavy-handed lobbying that went out the window every place but in Bloomington several years ago."[14]

Yet 300 people opted to attend the football weekend. They

listened to young Bloomington Mayor, Robert Benedict, tell them that the suburb was willing to contribute the 3 percent admissions tax (which then funneled directly into the general fund of Bloomington) to the costs of either remodeling the Met or building a new football stadium next to it. Benedict's offer was contingent on a citizens' referendum in the spring.

The fervid attempts of Bloomington civic leaders to keep the Vikings and the Twins in their area were propelled primarily by the intangible benefits the teams brought to the suburb. In 1974 the Bloomington chamber conducted a survey of area hotels and motels in order to assess the need for more accommodations. Established owners wanted the council to stop issuing permits for new motels and hotels. They were worried that Bloomington was overbuilding, in the fashion of cities like Orlando. The survey sought in part to identify the main sources of business for the suburb's hotels and motels. According to Benedict, they found that the airport brought in approximately 58 percent of the industry's business. Conventions accounted for 18 percent of their overnight guests. But sporting events brought in a mere 3.5 percent of the hotel and motel business.

The study did not intend to illustrate the city's relatively low dependency on the stadium. But it did make it embarrassing for Bloomington officials to argue for a suburban stadium on economic grounds. In fact many council members agreed that the city would make more money from taxes if the stadium land were developed for commercial purposes. Yet this did not detract from the intangible benefits city leaders felt the suburb derived from the stadium. The Vikings and the Twins were literally Bloomington's lease on national fame and glamour. Bloomington voters wanted to keep them. Bloomington politicians were prepared to fight for them. And now they had a place to plead their case.

## The Senators Ask for a Breather

On April 9, 1975, Minnesota Governor Wendell Anderson announced that he was convinced the Twins and the Vikings would leave the state if the legislature failed to pass a bill providing for a new or vastly remodeled stadium. If the legislators refused to satisfy the teams' demands, the governor predicted that "within the next couple of years we will lose the franchises. The people who own these franchises have made it very clear in their testimony before legislative committees that if they don't get a new stadium they will leave."[15]

In his testimony before the Senate subcommittee on Metropolitan and Urban Affairs, Vikings' General Manager Mike Lynn refused to release the team's financial statements. He did, however, inform committee members that the team's net profit in 1973 was slightly below the NFL average of $420,000 per club. He also testified that the Vikings would not sign a long-term lease for a modestly expanded Bloomington stadium.

By April of 1975 there were two stadium bills under committee consideration. One would allow the Hennepin County Board, with jurisdiction over both Minneapolis and Bloomington, to sell up to $65 million in general revenue bonds — backed by taxes on business property — to build a stadium. The other provided for the creation of a new Sports Commission, under the direction of the Metropolitan Council. It could decide whether to construct a new stadium or to expand either the Met or the University's Memorial stadium.

Some committee members were not convinced that the Vikings threats to abandon the area were real. Nor were they impressed by the feasibility study and the multi-purpose domed stadium recommendation of the downtown task force. A report released by the Senate staff was critical of the task force for "not being representative of the general public." "Even if the stadium can be built at the cost estimated by the task force (between $50 and $126 million)," the report stated, "it seems unlikely that any new or altered stadium could pay for itself."[16]

On April 9, 1975, the Senate subcommittee issued a position paper which maintained that the Twins and the Vikings provided both tangible and intangible benefits to the area. "We want the teams to stay in Minnesota," the committee members said, "and we must match that desire with the need for a new or altered stadium to keep those teams." But before the Legislature authorized the money to build a stadium, committee members wanted to be sure that the "results of such expenditure will benefit the public."[17] Urging a stadium financing-device other than residential property taxes, the subcommittee decided that the question of public financing should be studied between legislative sessions.

The expensive feasibility study and lavish football weekend appeared to have little impact on some of the more skeptical legislators. "This proposal for a new multi-purpose stadium is dead," said St. Paul Senator John Chenoweth, "and the reason is that taxpayers are unwilling to sign a blank check. We're interested in having the Vikings stay, but the question is, what is the price?"[18]

## Sword-rattling by Calvin and Max

What was the price to keep the Twins and the Vikings? According to their spokesmen — the Vikings' Mike Lynn and Twins' Clark Griffith — it was a new stadium. While Lynn and the younger Griffith made many visits to the state capitol, owners Max Winter and Calvin Griffith kept a relatively low profile. (In the case of the outspoken and sometimes bumbling baseball owner Griffith, stadium promoters' considered this absence a blessing). Originally the teams insisted that only a domed stadium would meet their needs. But after years of marathon legislative hearings and stacks of unsuccessful bills, they were ready to settle for considerably less, as long as it wasn't a remodeled Metropolitan or University of Minnesota stadium. "The idea of playing in the college stadium is even more repugnant than playing in Metropolitan stadium,"[19] declared Lynn.

While it was understandable that the Vikings objected to playing in a park built for baseball, it is not nearly as clear why the Twins were pressing for a Minneapolis domed stadium. One explanation is that Twins' officials worried about a possible legislative vote to build a football-only stadium. The Twins also were afraid that the Met would never be renovated. They favored a downtown site because of the more convenient location and the bus service available for people who were unable to attend games in Bloomington. Clark Griffith thought that a dome would help the Twin's attendance (although it might be argued that there are more notable ways to increase attendance, such as winning ballgames). "Consumers in the state of Minnesota are very weather conscious," Griffith observed. "Out in New York they mention that it might rain so a guy picks up an umbrella. That's the only difference in his life — one umbrella. Out here people just thrive on weather forecasts. They are always talking about the temperature and the expected precipitation. It cuts into our attendance. A dome eliminates the weather factor. It will bring more people to ballgames."[20]

The Vikings also argued for a dome on grounds that weather conditions kept fans away and too often made the game miserable for those brave creatures who did attend. But frozen weather had proved to be a plus for the football team in the past, especially when it played against teams whose players were accustomed to sensible field conditions. The infamous December tundra at the Met prompted Carroll Rosenbloom, owner of the Los Angeles Rams, to offer a private donation of $1,000 if and when the Minnesota legislature authorized a domed stadium. "It's a great team and a great part of the country," said Rosenbloom, whose beach-loving athletes were about to meet the Vikings in a December N.F.L. championship game. "But I don't think either the football teams or the fans ought to be subjected to the kind of weather conditions we might get Sunday in Minnesota."[21]

Playing indoors could reduce the Viking's competitive edge. The team had one of the worst records on artificial turf in the league. And, noted General Manager Lynn, in 50 years no team had lost every single home game except Seattle and New Orleans — both of which played under domes. Admittedly both teams were capable of losing all their home games in any environment.

So why were the Vikings lobbying for a Minneapolis stadium? "It certainly wasn't for economic reasons," says Lynn, "we would have been a lot better off in a new open-air stadium in Bloomington than in a downtown Minneapolis dome . . . our occupancy costs in Bloomington would have been zero."[22]

Lynn insists today that he favored an open-air stadium in

Bloomington. So did the Vikings' coach Bud Grant, who is renowned for braving the blizzards — the coach who refuses to allow his players to use sideline hand warmers or other alien forms of survival. "We would rather play on grass and under blue sky," said Grant. "I'm a grass man and like the open air . . . Maybe I'm old-fashioned."[23] Yet both Lynn and Grant eventually lobbied for the domed Minneapolis stadium. "I'm an employee of the club," Lynn explained. "If I'm going to object to anything I'll do it privately. In a corporate situation, once a decision is made, you have one of two choices: you either support that decision or you quit."[24]

So if it wasn't economic or competitive logic that dictated the Vikings' preference for a downtown dome over an open-air Bloomington stadium, what then?

Enter Max Winter. He grew up amid the delis of Minneapolis' North side. He stayed loyal to the city in its struggles. And while he was rarely accused of sentimentalism by his critics, he was sentimental about Minneapolis. This, in part, shaped his decision, according to Lynn.

And, from a more practical point of view, the Vikings probably had a better chance to secure a new stadium — domed or undomed — by siding with the Minneapolis people. "They wanted a new stadium and the momentum was clearly on the side of Minneapolis," noted Bloomington's Robert Benedict. "They felt it was better to go with the momentum."[25]

By 1976 the Vikings were creating some momentum of their own. Rumors were floating that the team had stadium offers from New York, Phoenix, and other unidentified cities. The mayor of Memphis offered to guarantee the team 72,000 "first-class seats" if the franchise moved to his city. It was becoming increasingly difficult for legislators to scoff at the teams' threats to move when many of their constituents believed them. A statewide poll conducted by the Minneapolis *Tribune* in March of 1976 found that 51 percent of Minnesotans thought a new stadium was needed to keep the Twins and the Vikings based in Minnesota, while only thirty-three percent of those polled disagreed with the statement.[26]

How real was the threat? "While there were available football stadiums," recalls Clark Griffith, "there were not any open baseball stadiums. There was one in Washington D.C., but as an American League team we couldn't go there because it fell within the geographic limits of the Baltimore franchise."[27] According to Mike Lynn, the Vikings gave some thought to relocating, but it was not until 1979 that they gave it serious consideration. "In the years between 1974 and 1977 we were looking into the possibility of relocating," he remembers, "but if you asked us what our chances would be of getting league approval for a move, I would say at the time they were pretty slim."[28]

Regardless of the veracity of the rumored threats, state legislators were, in the words of former Senator Steve Keefe, "caught in a kind of Catch-22....If we built the stadium no one would ever believe that the Vikings would have left and they'd be mad. If we didn't build the stadium they'd leave and people would be mad at us because we let them leave.....What do you do in a situation like that?"[29]


## A Pile-up at Mid-field

Up to now the lines for the legislative battle seemed straightforward enough. The teams were well-defined, the stakes clear-cut. On one side was the city of Bloomington, whose civic commanders were welded to the idea of holding onto the Twins and Vikings. In addition to their lavish "football weekend" they spent nearly $8,000 on a newspaper advertising campaign intended to entrench their cause. Leading the suburb in its stadium drive were Bloomington Chamber Vice President Donald Groen, assorted state legislators, and the energetic young mayor Robert Benedict, who, by virtue of his persistent attempts to thwart the Minneapolis domed stadium effort, evoked many wounded snarls from the downtown dome's proponents. "If it were allowable," said Vikings' General Manager Mike Lynn,

"I'd like to wring that little mayor's neck." [30]

Benedict and his cohorts were making life very unpleasant for Mike Lynn and the Vikings' management, who wanted nothing to do with a remodeled Metropolitan Stadium, a structure which Lynn once unblushingly referred to as "a piece of crap." Lynn was arduously lobbying, in the name of his company, for a domed stadium in Minneapolis. And a domed stadium in Minneapolis was something that the Minneapolis Chamber of Commerce, as represented by Harvey MacKay and his task force, and the Minneapolis City Council and its lobbyist, city clerk Lyle Schwarzkopf, had been plotting for years.

The scenario produced a battleground with the antagonists looking something like this: wearing Vikings' purple and business green, an alliance of the Minnesota Vikings, the Minnesota Twins, the Minneapolis political wheels, and the Minneapolis business people.

Wearing martyr-white, the defenders of Bloomington. Although the suburban knights lacked the war chest of their opposition, they were equally voluble. Railing against the "big city" and "big business," Bloomington leaders succeeded in portraying their city as the popular underdog.

But the conflict was more complicated than that. On the sidelines was a menagerie of fascinated watchers and agitators, many of whom were not especially concerned with the plight of the Vikings, the state of Minneapolis' development efforts, or the heroic postures of the Bloomington officials. But as the legislative battle became more intricate, as the issue became embroiled in the questions of *where* the stadium should be located and *who* should pay for it, the sidelines were quickly vacated. The battlefield soon swarmed with eager auxiliaries.

There was organized labor, led by David Roe, a long-time stadium advocate. The cigar-smoking, tough-talking Minnesota AFL-CIO president had all the trappings of a typical labor boss. But the man's devotion to labor was indestructible; and he was both an articulate and shrewd negotiator at the Capitol. In a legislature dominated by Democrats, Roe's stance, and more particularly labor's, had impact.

According to Roe, one reason a stadium would be an asset to labor was the construction and employment the project would provide. More importantly, anything that "increases the tax base and helps the community" would benefit labor. Roe had been lobbying for the stadium for 20 years. He was in on the drive to build Metropolitan stadium in 1955. His creed: "You just have to keep hammering away. It's like with Social Security and Medicaid and the laws to assure safety on the job. It has taken us almost thirty years to allow public employees some of the basic rights that their brothers and sisters have in the private sector. It takes persistency and it takes a continuous effort."[31]

While Roe had waged some stinging battles against business interests, labor and business were working together on the stadium issue, creating a kind of double crunch in lobbying legislators. "Basically the business community had influence with some legislators who wouldn't listen to us," said Roe, "and we had influence with some legislators who wouldn't listen to them."[32]

The pro-stadium alliance was not always unified, however. Sometimes signals got crossed. At one point Roe announced that "people close to the Vikings" told him that the team would move to Memphis if the legislature failed to authorize a new stadium. This news irritated Mike Lynn who wanted to avoid accusations that he was trying to blackmail the legislators into approving the stadium. Lynn declined "to dignify the rumor by commenting on it."[33]

The last thing Lynn wanted to do was to alienate legislators by making last minute threats that the team might leave. Such comments would have surely offended outstate legislators, who, although they professed disinterest on the issue, were a powerful force, representing half the state's population. But the rural lawmakers' "disinterest" in the stadium often translated into opposition to the project. To many in the farm country the stadium was just another frivolous "big city" project. "I would just as soon the teams moved to Washington," said a representative from Owatonna, "My people in southern Minnesota used to have tickets . . . they don't anymore."[34] Legislators from outlying areas were also irritated by the talk about implementing a hotel-motel tax to back the bond sale on the stadium. Fifty percent of metropolitan hotel and motel customers were Minnesotans from outstate areas.

One of the most ingenious justifications for an anti-stadium vote was put forth by a rural senator named Charles Berg: he was opposed to the Minneapolis stadium on navigational grounds. Mr. Berg, who hailed from the town of Chokio, 35 miles from the South Dakota border, told legislators that his constituents didn't like to drive into downtown Minneapolis and St. Paul "because they got lost."

Berg's claim prompted one Minneapolis *Star* columnist to test the senator's assessment of his constituents' directional skills. He decided to telephone some Chokio residents. "I don't have any trouble driving in Minneapolis," A.E. "Ervy" Nelson told the journalist, "I go to the Twin Cities pretty often. It's really not very complicated when you think about it. I mean it goes from here to here." The columnist was unable to locate one Chokio citizen who admitted having any difficulty navigating the distance between Chokio and Minneapolis. "I'm not surprised Berg gets lost in Minneapolis," answered one voter, "Berg is the typical confused politician. To drive from here to the next town he needs a directional beam from the highway patrol."[35]

Confusion ran rampant in the stadium controversy. In addition to the sprinkling of rural legislators who were vocal in their opposition to a domed stadium, and the representatives from the city of Bloomington, who were alternately pushing for remodeling the Met and building a new stadium right next to it, there were the opposing forces from St. Paul. While some of the St. Paul legislators were willing to put aside anti-Minneapolis instincts for the sake of a downtown stadium, others were not so conciliatory. Many of the legislators from St. Paul and its suburbs, particularly minority leader Robert Ashbach, preferred to move the Vikings and the Twins to a renovated Memorial stadium, located on the University campus in St. Paul.

Then there were the loyal fans who objected to a domed stadium because "baseball was meant to be played under the sun and stars," and football is "an outdoor sport." Although these people did not have a formal organization, they joined in the general clamor at the Capitol. A splinter from this group was the tailgaters, who objected to a downtown dome not so much because it limited their game-watching enjoyment (their zest for pre-game drinks had been known to impair their abilities to watch games and to even walk into the stadium), but because a downtown dome would not come equipped with a parking lot. A dark and gloomy ten-story ramp simply didn't harmonize with their idea of a Sunday afternoon at the ballpark.

The positioning of cars was also of paramount concern to another opposing faction — the Cedar Riverside Neighborhood Group. Members of this organization, whose neighborhood adjoined the proposed downtown site, complained that the potential parking, traffic, and air pollution damage outweighed any possible benefits a stadium might generate.

Battling alongside the neighborhood group was the hotel-motel industry, whose leaders claimed to support a new stadium, but were nevertheless lobbying hard against the hotel-motel tax proposed to finance it. They were frequently joined by the liquor lobbyists, who were scandalized by the notion of a drink tax.

But the pile-up was not yet complete. Another important cause made a late entry into the stadium derby: The Arts. Governor Wendell Anderson spearheaded a drive to include a special arts funding provision in the stadium financing in order to make the plan acceptable to arts aficionados. The stadium bill eventually included an arts appropriation.

They were certainly tenuous coalitions. One group included the Bloomington crusaders, outstate critics, and neighborhood activists. They were sometimes allied with assorted University of Minnesota regents and hotel-motel and liquor lobbyists. The other group was made up of Minneapolis business and civic leaders, top-level employees from the football and baseball companies, and an ardent labor activist. They were joined by the arts advocates.

Could Picasso have asked for more creditable allies?

## Down to the Fingernails

"The stadium was one of those issues which just kept percolating again and again," remembered Senator Steve Keefe. "You'd think you had it straightened out and then it would boil up again . . . there was always another fire to put out."[36] In September of 1975, after studying the issue for three months, a joint Senate-House subcommittee took the position that the Met was fine for baseball, and although better facilities were needed for football, no more than $30 million should be spent to either remodel an existing stadium or to build an open-air stadium.

The Minneapolis stadium forces were now under siege. They wanted to drum up enough support for the Minneapolis site before the issue came before the full legislature in the spring. City Clerk Lyle Schwarzkopf, Mike Lynn and Clark Griffith worked throughout the summer and fall of 1975 to convince legislators to support a Minneapolis dome. They were joined by chamber lobbyists William McGrann, Mike Berman, and John Birchford. Chamber executive director Charles Krusell, executive vice president Bower Hawthorne (vice-president of the *Star & Tribune*), and the task force's Harvey MacKay also lobbied furiously for the Minneapolis site. "Harvey did the most work of anyone," recalled Louis DeMars, City Council President at the time. "Sometimes he was more of a help than you wanted. But most of the time we couldn't have done it without him."[37]

Within a few months the group had obtained a pledge from the business community to buy and clear 30 to 34 acres of land for the stadium. The Vikings and Twins agreed to sign long-term leases for a downtown dome. In January of 1976 the subcommittee changed its original $30 million plan to one proposing a 65,000-seat multi-purpose stadium in Minneapolis. The $45 million stadium was to be financed with general obligation bonds. The bonds were to be repaid with stadium revenue. If revenue fell short, a 1.5 percent hotel-motel tax would make up the difference.

But by March of 1976 the subcommittee's January proposal was draped with so many amendments that it bore little resemblance to the original bill. One proposed a metropolitan-wide referendum on the stadium question. Governor Anderson's proposal for a $2.8 million arts appropriation was accepted. The 1.5 percent hotel-motel tax had been transformed in committee to a one percent cigarette tax, which was later removed and replaced by a one percent liquor tax, which ultimately was raised to a two percent liquor tax to be imposed only in the metropolitan area. The stadium legislation had been pronounced "dead" and "buried" so many times a letter to the editor in one newspaper suggested that it have a special spot in the Minnesota obituary listings.

Finally in April the House narrowly passed a stadium bill which included the arts appropriation and a two percent on-sale metropolitan-area liquor tax. A decision on the location of the stadium was to be made by a three-member arbitration panel appointed by the governor. Now the bill went to the Senate for approval.

On April 3, 1976, the Senate defeated the House bill by a vote of 37 to 21. Although Senate Democrats were divided on the issue, it was charged that some Republican senators had made the stadium a partisan issue. "Then the Republicans will say the Democratic legislature didn't do anything to keep the teams here,"[38] scowled one Democratic senator. Unable to secure enough votes to pass the House bill, Senate majority leader Nick Coleman tacked on a $100 million tax rebate bill which had been previously accepted by the Senate, but twice defeated in the House. Unrelated to the stadium question, the rebate would return 10 percent of the 1975 income taxes to the taxpayers. The Senate passed the stadium and tax rebate bill by a vote of 38 to 20. House leaders were vehemently opposed to the bill, however, on grounds that it could not be financed with the available budget surplus.

By attaching the tax rebate to the stadium bill, Coleman hoped to force the House to accept the rebate. "It's a bit of parliamentary trickery that makes no sense," said Senator Robert North, "If you are truly concerned about the taxpayers, lower taxes. Don't give a rebate in an election year."[39] Others marked

Coleman's move as an attempt to discreetly kill the stadium. Coleman was from St. Paul, and the old intercity suspicions were no myth. "If the bill couldn't have passed the Senate, fine," said House Speaker Martin Sabo, "those things happen. I would have preferred that they would have honestly dealt with it, instead of pretending to pass a bill when they were actually killing it."[40]

Coleman denied the charges that he had tied the rebate to the stadium bill in order to kill it for the session. "That's absolutely incorrect," he said, "There was no way on God's green earth that the stadium bill would have passed. At most it had thirty-one votes. I counted. It's chances were zero."[41]

Whatever the truth to the allegations, Coleman was right about the odds. Even though the bill managed to make it through the Senate, the House failed to approve it. The chances that the bill would pass the 1976 state legislative session were truly nil. The session was over.

## Somebody Call a Play!

Jimmy Carter's successful bid for the presidency in 1976 was enlightening to those convinced that a southerner would never be elected to the White House. But Carter's election set off some smaller tremors as well. Imagine the shock experienced by Minnesotans who woke up one morning to find their Scandinavian governor replaced by a Slavic dentist from the "Iron Range" town of Hibbing, Minnesota. In 1976 Minnesota's Senator Walter Mondale was elected to the vice presidency. It was the governor's responsibility to appoint his replacement. Wendell Anderson, a young and popular governor, decided that he was the most likely candidate for the post. He resigned as governor, an act that elevated Rudy Perpich, his lieutenant governor, to succeed him. Governor Perpich promptly appointed Wendell Anderson to fill the Senate vacancy. Perpich, a warm-hearted, easy-going populist Democrat, was ruled by two passions: one was his zest for politics, the other his love for polka parties.

Unlike his predecessor, Governor Perpich had expressed little interest in the stadium issue during his term as lieutenant governor. But the stadium was one of Anderson's favorite projects. After the bill's legislative defeat in April of 1976 Anderson had requested a $150,000 traffic and environmental stadium study. The proposed study was an unpopular one among legislators and the governor's request was not granted. As senator, Anderson continued to promote the stadium. Yet he had no formal authority over the project's outcome. But he obviously did have some influence with Rudy Perpich. Rudy Perpich began politicking for a new stadium.

There were also some changes in the stadium cast. Robert North, the Democratic state Senator from St. Paul who carried the bill in the last session, did not seek re-election. North returned to the ministry. Sponsoring the stadium bill in the Minnesota legislature evidently was enough to drive the devout back to the pulpit.

Mayor Robert Benedict survived the verbal bombast of Minneapolis critics. His relentless efforts on behalf of a Bloomington stadium made Benedict popular among his Bloomington constituents. The mayor was elected to the state senate in 1976. As senator, Benedict continued to trumpet the Bloomington stadium cause. He formed a "Committee to Let the People Decide." The group ran an advertisement in the *Star & Tribune* recommending that people send in a coupon requesting a citizen's referendum on the Stadium issue. The coupons were to be addressed to Senator Robert Benedict.

In the fall of 1976 Bloomington representatives presented another plan for an open-air football stadium in their suburb. The proposed 65,000-seat stadium was to built between the Met and the hockey rink. If adopted, this plan might have earned Bloomington a spot in the Guiness record book — not many other places could boast of three stadiums in one parking lot. The bill was sponsored by Senator William Kirchner, a representative from Richfield (a suburb which borders Bloomington) and Representative Bruce Williamson, a Democrat from Bloomington. The plan was endorsed by the chamber of commerces from the southern suburbs of Bloomington, Edina, Richfield, and Eden Prairie.

The Minneapolis City Council countered with a bill which called for a 65,000-seat domed stadium in their city. The bill was endorsed by none other than Mayor Charles Stenvig. After a brief return to his old job defending Minneapolis from crime, the burglary detective defied both Democratic and Republican critics by getting himself reelected in 1975. The Minneapolis bill was introduced in the House by Representative James Casserly, a Democrat from Minneapolis.

Senator Robert Ashbach, the Republican minority leader from the St. Paul suburb of Arden Hills, plagued both of the contending forces by introducing a bill to remodel and add a dome to the University of Minnesota stadium. There was also a plan for a $50 million, 70,000-seat domed stadium in the northern suburb of Coon Rapids.

If you didn't have a stadium proposal in Minnesota, you were a misfit. The plans were practically identical to those introduced the year before. And it looked as though the legislature was headed for another stadium debacle. But the 1977 legislators differed from their 1976 counterparts in one important respect. They had an election behind them. And after three years of stadium brawling the legislators were beginning to resent the enormous amount of time that had been spent on the issue. They wanted to get it settled.

But the morass was so deep it seemed almost impossible to ford. There was no forseeable way to make everyone happy. You couldn't build half of the stadium in Minneapolis and the other half in Bloomington. (One ingenous designer did come up with a plan for a mobile, inflatable stadium which could be transported from one site to another). "The problem with the stadium," in Senator Keefe's view, "was that there was no majority for any one position. A minority didn't want a stadium at all. A minority wanted it in Minneapolis. A minority wanted it in Bloomington. Ordinarily when you have legitimate differences you can find a middle ground, but in the case of the building of the stadium, it was strictly a yes/no proposition."[42]

Or was it?

## A Stadium, Finally. But Where?

On March 9, 1977 the House Local and Urban Affairs Committee met to hear bills on the stadium issue. Representative Al Patton, a Democrat from Sartel, got up and laid out a map of the Twin Cities metropolitan area before the committee members. He had an aide place a round glass ash tray atop the map. "This is a stadium," said the rural Minnesota legislator, "And as you see it will go just about anywhere on the map." Then Patton flipped the ashtray over. "And the same can be said of a domed stadium," he noted.

Patton's "ashtray" or "no-site" bill was as uncomplicated as the prop he had used to introduce it. The legislation would create a seven-member citizen's committee, appointed by the Governor, which would pick a site and a design for the stadium. "Basically this bill puts the legislators in the role of policy makers instead of architects," Patton explained. "If we're going to start arguing about which community needs the stadium most, whether it should be domed or not, what colors the seats should be painted, we're going to be right back to where we were two years ago and there won't be a stadium." Added the representative, "Frankly, this is the only bill that will fly."[43]

Patton's no-site stadium bill was engineered by Governor Perpich and the House and Senate majority leaders. (Senate majority leader) Coleman really wanted to get the issue out of the legislature," said Senator Keefe, "The no-site bill was his and (House majority leader) Sabo's idea to get the issue resolved. Sabo picked Patton to carry it in the House and Coleman had me carry it in the Senate."[44] By having Patton manage the bill, backers of the stadium were trying to ward off outstate opposition. According to Patton, he was asked to be the chief sponsor of the House bill because as an outstate representative he had "no commitment to units of local government."[45] Some rural legislators disliked the idea of spending more money on Minneapolis. They preferred a Bloomington site and might have voted against a "no-site" bill sponsored by two urban representatives. Remarked Senator Benedict, "A lot of the outstate people who decided to favor the no-site bill felt that the end result would be a Bloomington stadium. Otherwise they wouldn't have voted for it."[46]

On March 31 the no-site bill was put to vote in front of the Senate Government Operations Committee. Before Keefe could present the legislation, Senator William Kirchner of Richfield offered an amendment to give the stadium a site. He proposed that the stadium be located in Bloomington. The amendment passed by a vote of 8 to 7.

That the suburb of Bloomington received so much support from state legislators requires explanation. Many legislators who sided with the suburb did not want a stadium at all. By joining with the Bloomington backers, the anti-stadium legislators could make sure there would not be enough votes to pass either a Bloomington or Minneapolis bill. The strategy had worked for some time. But eventually, said Senator Jack Davies, a Minneapolis legislator who was opposed to the stadium, the opponents just got tired. "Those people (the stadium proponents) just kept pushing and pushing and pushing. You had to beat them 100 percent of the time. If you lost just once, the project would be authorized."[47]

The Bloomington bill was re-converted to a no-site bill in a Senate tax committee. On April 28 the bill came up on the Senate floor for a vote. There were enough Bloomington and Minneapolis stadium advocates to pass the no-site proposal. The question remained whether those advocates would split or pass the bill. Despite a late-hour attempt by Senator Robert Ashbach to outflank it with a bill calling for the renovation of the university stadium (that proposal failed by a narrow 30 to 31 vote), the Senate finally passed the no-site bill by a vote of 40 to 24.

The stadium bill was off to the House, where it had fizzled a year before. But after considering 20 amendments to the bill, the House adopted only five minor changes. It passed the no-site bill and the Senate agreed to accept the amendments. In its final form, the legislation provided for the creation of a seven-member citizens' commission, appointed by the governor, to select a site and design for the stadium. The stadium would be financed by revenue bonds. If revenue fell short, the difference would be made up through a two percent metropolitan-area liquor tax. The commission could spend no more than $55 million for the stadium's construction. It could spend up to $37.5 million if it chose to build a new football stadium in Bloomington and improve the Met for baseball; up to $25 million if it chose to remodel the Met as a multipurpose stadium; no more than $55 million if it decided to build a domed stadium. The legislative document was lengthy and inclusive. Its mandates ranged from affirmative action plans for building contractors to environmental impact studies for potential stadium sites.[48]

In May the bill was sent to Governor Perpich. "I'm happy the issue has finally been resolved," he said. "I'm convinced it was resolved in the best interest of the state." Surrounded by legislative leaders, representatives from both the Minneapolis and Bloomington chambers of commerce, and the owners and managers of the two sports teams, he signed the bill, handing out nearly two dozen pens in the process. "The reason I have all these people here is that I want them to share the credit," noted the governor, ". . . and the blame."[49] As a statement of unity, it seemed ironic enough to please all of the feudists.

After four years of heated legislative debate the stadium issue was "finally resolved."

Or was it? The stadium commission had the right to build a domed stadium if it wanted. It could build an undomed stadium. It could build a stadium anywhere in the metropolitan area. On the other hand, it might not want to build a stadium at all. It had the option to remodel the Met. While the legislators authorized that something *could* be done, they were unable to decide where or how it should be done. To their credit, they did come up with a financing plan. The detailed legislation was specific and binding. But the real choices would be made by seven people, citizens not electorally beholden to the public.

The legislators had completed a pass.

Rudy Perpich

Nick Coleman

Calvin Griffith

Clark Griffith

"When the stadium was debated in the Minneapolis council the major question was whether or not it would be good for the city . . . but when the stadium got into the legislature, the questions became more complicated . . . we were asking not only if there should be a stadium, but also where it should be located and who should pay for it."[1] — Steve Keefe

# 4

# THE INTEREST GROUP BATTLE

In 1973 the stadium project became a matter of state rather than local concern.[2] No longer was the stadium defined simply as an urban development project; it became entangled in statewide interest group politics. It was not just the shift to a different level of government which complicated the issue — urban controversies can be as intricate and turbulent as those at the state level. After three years of city council debates, the project practically demanded intervention from forces outside the urban domain.

Although the question of whether a new sports arena was in the public interest continued to punctuate the politicians' rhetoric, other questions gained priority: should the stadium be built in Bloomington or Minneapolis? Should it be domed or undomed? Should its financing be backed by a tax on cigarettes or on hotel rooms? From 1970-1973 the stadium was best understood as a problem to which a government responded. From 1973-1977 it was a project over which interest groups battled. The legislature's final decision was not so much a *choice* or a *response*, as it was a *resultant* of the political process.[3]

The no-site bill which the Minnesota legislature passed in 1977 was the result of years of interest group bargaining. The groups involved in the controversy, the influence they wielded, the power structure they worked in — these are the factors which explain how the conflict was finally resolved.

## Political Interest Groups

Suppose that a person living in the Cedar-Riverside neighborhood, the area which adjoins one of the proposed downtown sites, is worried that traffic from a new stadium will endanger the lives of his children. There will be an influx of cars, and some of the drivers will be drunk. The man calls up the woman down the block who is a member of the Cedar-Riverside Neighborhood Group. He tells her why he is opposed to a new stadium. At the next meeting members discuss the issue. Several people have approached them with fears of traffic and parking problems that would result from a nearby stadium. The residents' complaints are generalized so that they can be asserted as one well-defined claim: the Cedar-Riverside Neighborhood Group is opposed to a new stadium because it will create parking, traffic, and environmental problems in its neighborhood.

The politics of public interest require "generalization."[4] Individuals who wish to participate in the political process generalize their interests by identifying them with certain groups. Thus an "interest group" is simply "a number of individuals with a common interest."[5] Two kinds of groups participate in the political process. Permanent groups, such as the Minneapolis Chamber of Commerce and the AFL-CIO, participate in a wide range of issues. They are fixtures of the political process. Ad hoc groups, such as Sen. Benedict's "Committee to Let the People Decide," and Harvey MacKay's stadium task force, are formed to participate in a certain issue.

## Resources and Strategies

Government actions result from the pushing and pulling of interest groups. Each group tries to influence decision-makers to adopt proposals favorable to the group's interest. Influence is the "ability to get others to act, think, or feel as one intends."[6] Influence determines how a policy or project originates, how it is considered, how its decision is formulated, how it is amended and implemented. The outcome of a conflict is contingent on the relative influence exerted by contending sides.

The extent of a group's influence depends partly on its resources. Money, information, time, prestige, numbers, tactical skills and allies all constitute political resources. The wealth of the Minneapolis Chamber of Commerce, for instance, was a critical resource. It allowed the chamber to buy another resource, information, in the form of the $25,000 feasibility study. The study was provided to the decision-makers in an attempt to promote the chamber's interest. For David Roe and the members of the AFL-CIO, strategically placed allies (legislators on key committees who were responsive to the wishes of labor) were an important resource. Housing the Vikings allowed Bloomington officials to lobby legislators with their "football weekend."

But influence is not only dependent on resources. A group's strategies and skills also determine its effectiveness. Bloomington pursued a strategy of "appealing to the people" by frequently calling for metro and statewide referendums on the stadium issue. In order to ward off criticism that he was trying to "blackmail" legislators into adopting a stadium proposal, Mike Lynn tried to silence talk of the team's possible departure. The "no-site" bill was a strategic move on the part of House and Senate leaders to get the general issue of a sports stadium resolved and out of the legislature.

Finding allies is a strategic necessity in a contentious public controversy. This is part of the reason that the Vikings and Twins worked so closely with the Minneapolis business interests. "They wanted a new stadium and the momentum was clearly on the side of Minneapolis . . . They felt it was better to go with the momentum."[7] Strategically it benefited the teams to join forces with the Minneapolis interests.

On the other side were those opposed to a new stadium regardless of where it would be built. For this group, a fruitful strategy was to promote the proposal which had the least chance of passing at any particular time. Sometimes the stadium objectors would vote with the Bloomington advocates, other times they would opt for the University stadium renovation. The course of their strategy depended on which bill would defeat the favored proposal without acquiring enough support to pass itself.

Another strategy employed by political groups is to claim the "public interest" value of their stance. Their position is taken not only to further their own interest, but also to enhance the public interest. This technique was used by all of the stadium participants. "The general public should be given the chance to vote in a referendum."[8] "Putting the stadium downtown provides much greater opportunities for poor and old people, for blacks, for people without cars."[9] The stadium will "increase the tax base and help the community."[10]

Treating this strategy as a "technique" does not imply that such claims are necessarily fictitious. It is frequently impossible to distinguish between private-serving and community-serving activity. Often one benefits the other. But nevertheless the tendency for advocate groups to emphasize a certain aspect of the public interest, for leaders to "stand up" for a certain conception of the public interest, is a useful political tool.

## The Structure of Power

Democracy means rule by the people. But when less than one percent of the people exercise inordinate influence in a democracy, it raises serious questions as to the reality of the democratic creed. It is rare that bargaining resources of conflicting interests are equal. Participation in the American political system is usually marked by a strikingly unequal distribution of resources.

Those who control an area's businesses, the people who serve on corporate and community boards, possess political resources unavailable to the average citizen. Because of their prestige, elites can be assured that their remarks and opinions will be published in the newspaper. They are able to contribute large amounts of money to election campaigns. Their circumstances permit them to devote more time to issues than people who are tied to nine-to-five jobs. Their money can buy information to sway elected officials.

Do these resources allow the business elite to control local politics in America? In his study of government in Atlanta, Floyd Hunter found that the economic and social elites constituted a "community power structure" that essentially ran the town. These elites were the "dominant policymaking group" who used the "machinery of government as a bureaucracy for the attainment of certain goals coordinated with their interests."[11] Their resources enabled top business leaders to "enforce their decisions by persuasion, intimidation, coersion, and if necessary force."[12] Hunter popularized the "elitist" theory of government action. Influence is in the hands of a certain group which has maintained its power position over the years. Despite the proliferation of interest groups there is still an "elite" group which dominates the government.

Do we conclude that a small group of people have ample power to determine the outcome of most public issues in American politics?. One of the quarrels with Hunter's study is that in asking Atlanta community members "who" they thought belonged to the city's power elite, he assumed the existence of a power elite. While there may well be a community "elite," a capacity or willingness to exercise power is not necessarily part of its character. Those with money and prestige do have a greater chance to influence decision-making than the average citizen. This does not mean that they are a unified group with a common set of goals. Their ability to wield power does not imply they will always do it. Nor can one infer that elected officials will respond positively to these elite preferences.

The elite are not always unified. In the case of the stadium project, certain businessmen "by and large liked the way things were in Bloomington and saw no particular reason to change things."[13] Although these business opponents did not spend the time or resources of their colleagues who wanted the downtown dome, the Minneapolis business community was far from unified on the stadium issue.

Generally speaking, some members of a city's business elite may lack interest in the outcome of local disputes, particularly people who represent national firms headquartered in the community. In the Minneapolis stadium controversy the majority of those who headed the Minneapolis-based national firms showed little enthusiasm for the conflict. "They were less concerned with local developmental issues"[14] than were the locally-oriented business people. While the presidents of national companies were certainly capable of exerting influence, they chose not to do so.

Business people are more influential in some situations than they are in others. They tend to have more influence on issues where their objectives are compatible with those of elected officials and on issues which are not publicly prominent. "Businessmen are likely to have the greatest degree of success on low visibility issues," writes Demetrios Caraley in his study of urban government, "where the money cost to the city for complying with their claims is low, where potential opposition to the objectives fails to develop."[15]

Even if a "community power structure" ran government in Atlanta, Hunter's findings cannot be generalized to explain the workings of other local governments. Cities vary greatly as to what interests are influential in policy-making. And even in a political system in which the business elite is capable of exerting great influence, its ability to prevail depends on the unamimity of its goals, the visibility of the issue, and the forseeable benefits of its involvement.

An alternate theory, that of pluralism, holds that power is diffused among many different interest groups, and not the preserve of a single economic elite. "Far from being a ruling group," writes Robert Dahl in his study of New Haven politics, "the [economic elite] are simply one of the many groups out of which individuals sporadically emerge to influence the politics and acts of city officials."[16] Dahl emphasizes the importance of the processs by which decisions are made. In an open, pluralist political system, government actions are best explained by the struggles between groups.

The outcome of the three-year legislative stadium struggle supports the pluralist view. In spite of all of the maneuvering and meddling of the Minneapolis business corps, the outcome of the controversy was only partially favorable to its interest. The fact that the legislation took so long to pass — that it was stalled over and over again — surely demonstrates that the Minnesota legislature was not controlled by a behind-the-scenes power elite. And the legislation that finally passed, a bill which left the question of site location undecided, demonstrates that business wishes were not omnipotent.

One criticism of the pluralist doctrine is that it may overlook how an issue arrives on a government's agenda. In the case of the stadium, it was not only the owners of the sports establishment and the business leaders who advocated a new stadium, but also the members of the Minneapolis City Council. And after five years of debate, two years in the City Council and three years in the state legislature, the final outcome reflected the mix of groups party to the deliberations. The Vikings and Twins were promised either a vastly remodeled Met or a new stadium. Bloomington and Minneapolis civic leaders were partially appeased. The bill contained a provision that 10 percent of stadium contracts should be awarded to small businesses. Every business involved in the construction and maintenance of the stadium was required to have an affirmative action plan. The legislation stipulated that an environmental impact statement must be drawn for each alternative site. It contained a back-up liquor tax to protect residential property owners from unexpected costs. Two of the seven commission members were to be appointed from outstate.

No single power elite would engineer such legislation. Every group involved in the controversy left its stamp on the final bill. But because there was such a proliferation of interest in the battle, because so many people had access to the decision-making process, the issue just narrowly missed a fourth round in the legislature. And the fact that the hardest decision, the choice of a site, had to be delegated to people outside of the formal political system, illuminates the shortcomings of interest group pluralism. Elected politicians were unable to resolve the stadium conflict within the legislative body. Perhaps this was a victory for pluralism, but it was a defeat for democratic accountability. The people designated to settle the most hotly contested issue — that of location — would not have to answer to the public.

## Delegated Decision-Making

That so many groups were able to participate in the stadium controversy, that a myriad of interests had actual impact on the legislative outcome, shows us that pluralist democracy is not a facade. At least on this particular issue, many interest groups were able to exert political influence.

But it is this very openness, this frenzied and chaotic atmosphere, which makes it difficult to resolve conflicts in a pluralist democracy. Elected officials fall into the role of balancing competing interests rather than concerting unified action. Within this cacophonous bargaining game of American politics, it is virtually impossible to mobilize agreement on any public issue. Any time the number of disputants increases, the chances for a decision decreases. As more people became involved in the stadium controversy, as the arts advocates, neighborhood activists, and hotel-motel lobbyists began knocking on the legislators' doors, it became harder and harder to resolve the conflict.

The stadium controversy came to be a battle over "side" costs and benefits. Even if a majority of the legislators agreed that building a new stadium would be a positive public act,[17] they disagreed on who should be taxed for it and where it should be located.

The direct benefits and costs were clear: A new stadium would insure that the teams remained in Minnesota. If the legislators failed to provide them with a new or vastly remodeled facility, there was a chance they would leave the area.

The side costs and benefits were not so clear. Legislators argued over who should bear the support costs — the cigarette industry, the hotel-motel industry, or the bar-owners. They also debated whether the tax should be borne by the state, the city, or the seven-county metropolitan area. They questioned which locality would benefit more from a stadium. Who would incur the costs if a stadium was built in Minneapolis — the city of Bloomington, the adjoining neighborhoods, or the diehard tailgaters?

Disagreement over side costs and benefits is a common characteristic of political disputes involving public projects. When community residents decide that they need a new park, every neighborhood offers irrefutable proof that it and the park would form a union blessed by heaven. On the other hand, if a majority of community members agree that a new prison is necessary, no one wants it in his back yard.

How are these seemingly irreconcilable conflicts resolved? Sometimes a powerful politician or political party or interest group may engineer a project through the workings of government. In other cases, the coordinating authority is delegated to a non-elected administrative agency. This is what happened with the Minnesota stadium controversy in 1977. By "passing the buck" the legislators were able to overcome the dispersed and decentralized immobility of the political process.

Although the citizens' commission began with an aura of apolitical cleanliness, the decision they would have to make was undeniably political. Someone would win. Someone would lose. The delegation of authority to "keep things moving," is inevitable in a system such as has been described here. But it signifies a tradeoff. The Minnesota legislature sacrificed accountable decision-making for political efficiency — and some degree of political sanity.

STADIUM BONDS

PROPOSED COVERED STADIUM
RICHARD GUINDON and ASSOC.
MINNEAPOLIS TRIBUNE 12 14

12-14-75
Minneapolis Star and Tribune

John Cowles, Jr.

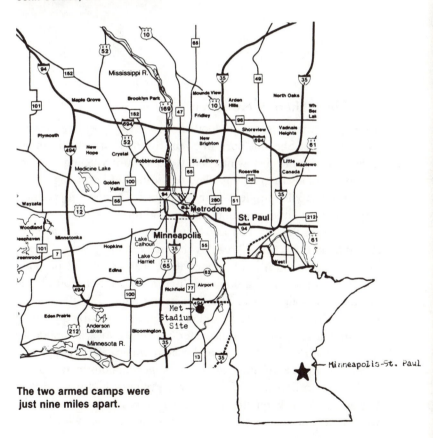

The two armed camps were
just nine miles apart.

85

"I didn't know Dan Brutger from page eight in an anatomy book." — Rudy Perpich of the man he picked to run the stadium commission

# 5

# THE STADIUM: 1977-1978

## And Then There Were Seven

Solveig Premack is not a football fan. Nor does she collect baseball cards. She was born in Sven, Sweden, and would much rather spend a blustery winter's day cross-country skiing through the north woods than ogling televised football in her living room.

A Minneapolis resident active in state Democratic politics, Premack paid little attention to the stadium promoters' seven-year siege on the city hall and state capitol. She served as vice-chairman of the Capitol Area Architectual Planning Board during most of the stadium battle. Since there was no official proposal for the construction of a domed coliseum on Capitol grounds she had neither obligation nor interest in the issue. But if someone had actually advanced such a plan, Premack undoubtedly would have handled it with aplomb. Her warmth and self-confidence give Solveig Premack a calm and easy manner. She is adaptable.

Sure evidence of this quality was her appointment to the stadium commission in May of 1977. Premack had worked with Governor Perpich on the architectual planning board when he was lieutenant governor. She was also acquainted with Senate majority leader Nick Coleman, one of the people who suggested that she be appointed to the commission. "I had never attended a Twins or a Vikings game," she admitted in an agreeable Swedish accent, "but you don't have to be a jock to build a stadium."[1]

For many years Solveig Premack had lived a perfectly healthy life without stepping inside a sports arena. She might have memorized the Minnesota Orchestra schedule but she could not tell her friends whether the Minnesota Vikings played in Detroit or Dublin. In fact on that memorable evening in May of 1977 she was getting ready to attend a concert.

"Mother," yelled one of her children, "Telephone!"

Solveig Premack was taking a bath.

"Who is it? I'm in the tub."

"You better hurry up . . . It's the Governor's office . . . It's something about a stadium."

Such was Solveig Premack's initiation into the stadium fraternity. Perpich wanted individuals who had not previously been involved with the controversy and who had never publicly expressed preferences on the issue. He wanted the commissioners to be politically "clean." Solveig Premack met all three requirements.

Premack was a refreshing addition to a controversy dominated by professional politicians, experienced lobbyists, and wealthy business boosters. Up to 1977, no woman had played a consequential role in the issue. Although by law he was only required to make the commission representative on a geographic basis, Perpich wanted it to be demographically diverse. "Perpich felt very strongly about having women and minorities in government," recalled Premack. "He wanted these groups to be represented on the commission."[2] The Governor also hoped that t! ommission would include a labor representative, a lawyer, and a person familiar with metropolitan government.

The legislation mandated the appointment of two of the seven commission members from outside of the Twin Cities. One was to be chosen from St. Paul, one from Minneapolis, one from the southern metropolitan suburbs, and one from the northern suburbs. Originally the chairman was to come from anywhere in the metropolitan area, but that was changed to anywhere outstate so that no area with a potential site would have two commissioners.

Perpich set up a "commission committee," composed of staff members, that asked legislators for their advice on appointments and made recommendations to the Governor. They never questioned the prospective appointees as to their site preferences, however. "We never tried to control where the stadium would go," said Perpich. "Personally I liked the downtown site because I thought it was good for the central city . . . But I had no idea how the vote would go."[3]

According to Solveig Premack, the Minneapolis appointee, none of the commissioners was sure of the final outcome either. "I think many Minneapolis people, especially the businessmen and politicians, took me as an automatic Minneapolis vote," she said. "That wasn't true . . . because I really didn't care what they thought of me. I was independent. There's not really much they could have done to me. They might not pick up my garbage, but that's about the worst they could do."[4] Unlike some of the other commission members, Premack had never held an elected office. Her husband, Frank, who was city editor with the Minneapolis *Tribune,* died in 1975. Although she had strong sentiments for Minneapolis, Premack never considered the city's residents to be her constituents.

St Paul appointee Richard Radman, on the other hand, seemed to have a different conception of his appointment. "Radman had more of a constituency than anyone else," said Dan Brutger, the commission's chairman. "In fact, I viewed him as the only member who had a constituency. St. Paul was very important to him and he had been a lifetime labor leader."[5] Radman was vice-president of the Minnesota AFL-CIO, the organization of which stadium promoter Dave Roe was president. Yet Radman was also Secretary and Business Representative of the St. Paul Building and Construction Trades Council. He lived and worked in St. Paul. He voiced the city's concerns at commission meetings. He considered himself the city's delegate on the commission.

Originally Perpich asked James Shannon, former auxiliary bishop of the Twin Cities Archdiocese, to serve on the commission. But Shannon was executive-director of the Minneapolis Foundation. Those opposed to a Minneapolis stadium were outraged. They accused Perpich of stacking the appointments in favor of Minneapolis. The Governor's office later announced that Shannon would not be serving on the commission.

"About this same time," remembered Solveig Premack, "Perpich realized that he didn't have a black on the commission. It would have been easier for him to choose a black from the cities, but he was left with the southern suburbs because he was sure of everyone else."[6] The Governor's staff located a suburban commissioner who met Perpich's requirements, however. Marion Kennon was a black resident of Edina, one of the Twin Cities' wealthiest suburbs. An elementary school teacher at Breck, a private school in the area, Kennon had less time to devote to the commission than other members because of the time constraints imposed by her job. She was described by Chairman Brutger as "bright" and "hard-working," however. "Like the other commissioners," he said, "I had full trust in her judgment."

Josephine Nunn, the third woman appointee, was characterized by a fellow commission member as "one of the brightest politicians I've ever worked with."[7] An active Democrat, Nunn was Mayor of Champlin, a small suburb northwest of Minneapolis. As a member of the Metropolitan Council's advisory committee on municipalities, Nunn brought to the commission a familiarity with metropolitan government. Nunn was the only commission member holding elected public office at the time of the appointments.

Kelly Gage, a lawyer from the southern Minnesota town of Mankato, was one of Perpich's outstate appointments. Gage served as a Republican Senator, representing the Blue Earth County District, from 1966 to 1972. "Perpich needed someone from the southern part of the state," said Gage. "People knew me because I had been U.S. Congressman Tom Hagedorn's campaign manager. Perpich and I had gotten along well in the legislature. I assume he wanted to balance the commission with a Republican appointment. I was it."[8] Perpich had also stipulated that he wanted to appoint a lawyer to the commission. Gage's credentials were impressive. That year he was elected president of the Minnesota State Bar Association.

Although he had not held elected office for five years, Gage retained a politician's instincts for delegated responsibility. He did not approach his appointment in an "apolitical" or "neutral" manner. Gage explained: "Being from southern Minnesota, Perpich might have guessed that I would have voted for Bloomington. The site was more accessible for the people from the southern part of the state. I think I had a bias towards Bloomington because of this. No one ever asked me. I think I tried to listen in an impartial way to presentations."[9]

Perpich acknowledged that he and his staff members had discussed how some of the appointees might vote. "Kelly Gage," he said, "we knew he was opposed to the Minneapolis site . . . Radman, being a labor man, we thought he'd go for downtown . . . Premack — we were pretty sure that she would vote downtown. But we never talked with any of them about it."[10]

The only other vote which Perpich felt he could predict was Ronald Gornick's. An outstate appointee from northern Minnesota, Gornick was a service station and motel owner in Chisholm, a small town on Minnesota's mining range. He had served on Wendell Anderson's Small Business Task Force and was a close friend of Perpich. "We're from the same neck of the woods and you figure a guy from the Iron Range would just as soon have a stadium downtown as in the suburbs," said Perpich. "Gornick was aware of what I wanted. That might have been enough."[11]

While Perpich was a close acquaintance of one commission member, he didn't know the commission's chairman "from page eight in an anatomy book."[12] Terry Montgomery, the governor's executive secretary who came from St. Cloud, recommended Dan Brutger, also of St. Cloud, for the chairmanship. "I didn't know anything about the stadium issue before I was selected," Brutger acknowledged. "I've never been active in politics . . . I'm a builder and I have a record of getting things done right and on time . . . People in the governor's office knew about my reputation."[13]

Brutger got his first job as a construction worker in St. Cloud, a town 80 miles northwest of the Twin Cities, when he was 15. After putting himself through college and working at Honeywell for a few years, he founded a construction company in 1954. The St. Cloud company, which eventually included the 28-member Thrifty Scot Motel Chain, grew to employ 650 people in 11 states. Brutger also bought a 63,000-acre Montana cattle ranch.

Dan Brutger found in the commission chairmanship a sudden and visible business challenge, a job that was sure to test all of his organizational and creative abilities. Perpich found in Brutger a strong and efficient chairman, a man "tailor-made for the job."[14] Perpich had wanted the appointed commissioners to be both conscientious and broadly representative. This he achieved. He chose a millionaire and a small-town mayor. He appointed a black and a labor leader. He picked someone who managed a winning congressional campaign and someone who managed a construction empire. He found people who belonged to every group from Planned Parenthood to the Moose Lodge.[15]

The commissioners had eighteen months to determine if and where a new stadium should be built. For the past eight years, answers to these questions had eluded thirteen puzzled aldermen, swarms of civic do-gooders, and over 200 boggled legislators.

And now only seven would decide.

## The Art and Craft of Stadium Planning

"None of us knew a thing about stadiums. That was a virtue, not a vice. It meant that we asked questions. It meant that we were open-minded."          — Donald Poss

A month after the governor appointed the commission, its members named Donald Poss as their executive director. Poss would not have a vote in the site decision. It was his job to coordinate the commissioners' work, to gather data, and to help the seven members to make an informed decision. Poss never advocated a specific site. "It was my practice not to make recommendations during the process," he said. "To this day my wife doesn't know what my choice might have been."[16]

Suggested by Josephine Nunn, Poss was serving as the Brooklyn Center city manager when the commission appointed him. With a degree in civil engineering, he was hired as the suburb's public works manager in 1960. Six years later the Brooklyn Center city council appointed him city manager. "Don Poss was one of the top city managers in the state . . . in the country, probably," remembered a former Brooklyn Center mayor. "He did his job well, fairly, and honestly. He treated every dollar as if it were his own, and he worked away until he felt the job had been done right."[17]

Poss had never built a public works project the magnitude of a $55 million stadium. He was a bureaucratic sophisticate who loathed the word "bureaucrat," and considered himself a "business manager" instead. Poss had full faith in his abilities to accomplish such a large-scale project. "If a manager from one industry is recruited into a completely different industry, as is often the case in the private sector," he said, "he already knows how to manage. The first thing he does is learn about the industry."[18]

Donald Poss learns quickly. Soon he was renowned for his command of stadium technology and budget statistics. The executive director's first task was to structure the commission. "It was like creating a new city or a new government," he said. "I had to start from scratch to set up the operating bylaws and the financial system." Poss also outlined the legislative mandates. "There were some rather tight time strings," he remembered. "We had to learn a lot about stadiums in a very short time."[19]

The commission's first assignment was to complete a review of candidate sites. Members took the position that rather than the commission looking for potential sites, the developers and interested communities could contact them. They would accept proposals up to June 27. According to the stadium bill, by August 1 they should have narrowed their choices to no more than three prospective sites.

By the June deadline, eight proposals had been submitted. Two of them were in Minneapolis: the site of the original City

Council plan (which was still without a parking ramp) and the Industry Square proposal. There were entries from Brooklyn Center, Coon Rapids and Bloomington. With the Minnesota Kicks soccer team gaining popularity in the area, one proposal called for a soccer-only stadium in St. Paul. A group of businessmen known as "Minnesota Dome Stadium Inc." submitted the final plan: it called for a stadium in the "Midway area" between Minneapolis and St. Paul.

Two proposals which had been previously discussed were not submitted to the commission. One plan — to remodel the University of Minnesota's Memorial Stadium — was rejected in April when the commission found that it would cost $20 million extra to accommodate the University requirements for recreational and intramural athletics. The other plan which failed to make the commission's deadline had been promoted by a firm calling itself "New Jerusalem Life Style and Air Mattress Company" (NJLSAMC). This group claimed it could solve the stadium problem by designing a portable, inflatable arena that could be carried from city to city on a truck. In other words, they were proposing an un-stadiumed dome. Ideally football fans could watch the first half of a Viking's game in Minneapolis and then move to Bloomington for the second half. If the Vikings were to leave the area, the stadium could go with them. Thus the city wouldn't be stuck with an empty "white elephant" arena. "We're as serious as the rest of the developers who have submitted proposals,"[20] noted Peter Kramer, an NJLSAMC spokesman.

While some of the developers may not have been entirely serious, the people who lived in neighborhoods adjoining potential sites were always earnest. In reaction to the Midway site, some Prospect Park residents mounted a campaign against the proposed stadium in their area. "The parking, litter, noise and bands of people would destroy one of the city's older residential neighborhoods,"[21] said the organizer of a letter-writing campaign against the site. Eventually the St. Paul City Council turned down the Midway proposal. The Council objected to the plan primarily because of the cost of street improvements needed to service the stadium.

One by one the potential stadium sites were either discarded because they failed to meet the legislative cost limits or withdrawn because of neighborhood dissent. "I've been a builder all my life . . . and I know that there are a lot of good projects that never get built because neighborhoods won't accept them," remarked Chairman Brutger. "Wherever there's change there's controversy. You could try to put a cathedral in a Catholic neighborhood and they'd object to the fact that when the priest pontificates there's too much traffic."[22]

By August 1 the commission had narrowed the plans down to three: Bloomington, Industry Square in Minneapolis, and Eagan, a suburb southeast of Minneapolis. The Eagan arena was to be built on a field owned by Dayton-Hudson Corporation. Developers envisioned the stadium as part of a massive shopping center. Most members of the Eagan community did not share the developers' visions. During public hearings, city council members decided that a stadium in their area would be unlikely to attract development. Declaring that Eagan couldn't afford to be the host city for the stadium, the city asked that the site be withdrawn from consideration.

Perhaps it was inevitable that the commissioners would be left with two choices — Bloomington and Minneapolis. And three figures: $37.5 million for an open-air football and soccer stadium in Bloomington; $42 million for an open-air multi-purpose stadium in Bloomington; $55 million for a domed multi-purpose stadium in Minneapolis. Because of the high water table in Bloomington, which would require that a dam be built around the stadium's base, the commission could only afford to build an open-air stadium in the suburb. And even in Minneapolis, where the water table was substantially lower, there was a good chance that it would not be feasible to build a dome within the allotted budget.

According to architect John Merrill of Skidmore, Owings, and Merrill, the firm the commission had hired to prepare stadium designs, it would be very difficult to build a domed stadium in Minneapolis. The $55 million limit imposed by the legislature was simply too low. None of the three multipurpose covered stadiums which Merrill had studied came close to meeting the limit set by the Minnesota legislature. The least expensive, the Astrodome in Houston, would cost $88 million to duplicate in 1979 prices. There was a chance, however, that an inflated-fabric rather than concrete-covered dome could be built for under $55 million in Minneapolis.[23]

Even with a nylon roof, it would be extremely hard to stay within budget. Only a few stadiums in the country had managed to keep a lid on expenses. The stadium commission embarked on a series of stadium tours to find out why. They went to Houston. They went to Dallas and Seattle. They went almost every place where a new stadium had been built in recent years except New Orleans. "There was absolutely nothing we could learn from that disaster," noted Solveig Premack, "except how not to do things . . . they are still losing enormous amounts of money."[24]

The commissioners spoke with stadium managers and staff. They looked at their audits and operations, "trying to extract what they did right and reject what they did wrong."[25] According to executive director Poss, the major defect in most of the stadium commissions and authorities across the country was that they were composed of individuals whom he referred to as "jock types." "They're enthralled with professional sports," Poss maintained. "They are willing to build at any cost . . . they cowtow to pro sports owners in lease negotiations."[26]

Not one of the Minnesota commissioners could be character-ized as a "jock type." In fact the group had an almost self-righteous attitude about their "non-jock" identity. They would not be manipulated by the teams' owners or by Minneapolis business lobbyists. "We set down the rules," said Premack. "They could testify at public hearings and that was it."[27]

While the hearings served as useful forums for Bloomington and Minneapolis leaders to testify, they were, according to many of the commissioners, worthless in assessing public opinion. "The hearings were the only legal requirement which really wasn't helpful,"[28] remarked one member. The commission was required to hold a series of ten public hearings, mostly outstate, for the purpose of gauging public sentiment towards a sports facility. "There were always more of us than there were of them," recalled Kelly Gage. "I was at one down in Marshall where there were only two people and the janitor who opened the building."[29] According to Gage, outstate people really didn't care about the issue. Minneapolis neighborhood groups, on the other hand, were extremely vocal during the public debates.

One particularly passionate group called itself "Save the Met." In sharp contrast to the business-suited Minneapolis and Bloomington spokesmen, this organization's members appeared at hearings in blue jeans and "Save the Met" t-shirts. "Sports were meant to be played outdoors," declared Julian Empson, the group's young leader. "Can you imagine the Minnesota Vikings playing inside in December wearing short-sleeve shirts?" he asked. "They'd have to change their names — call themselves the Minnesota Pussycats or something. They wouldn't be the Vikings of old."[30]

Public opinion bolstered Empson's charges. While in April of 1978, 77 percent of 614 Minnesotans interviewed agreed that the stadium was a "worthwhile project,"[31] six months later in a similar survey, only 38 percent of those interviewed agreed that a new stadium should be built. 42 percent felt that it should not be built. When asked which location and design they would favor if the commission chose to build a new stadium, 34 percent wanted a football/soccer domed stadium in Bloomington. 30 percent preferred an open air stadium in Bloomington. Only 30 percent were in favor of a domed stadium in Minneapolis.[32]

A 1974 Chamber of Commerce survey backed the 1978 results. The Chamber hired a national polling firm to conduct in-depth interviews throughout the state. According to Mike Lynn, the extensive survey, which was never made public, "proved conclusively that Minnesotans were in favor of the Bloomington site."[33]

Throughout the 1970's, the Minnesota public appeared to favor keeping the stadium in Bloomington. The majority of the Met Stadium customers objected to a new stadium in Minneapolis. St. Paul residents were instinctively opposed to a Minneapolis arena, both on traditional grounds of envy, and because it was a potential competitor to its Civic Center, which was used for hockey, basketball, shows, and conventions. The Minneapolis public itself, as distinct from the civic promoters, showed a mixture of support, indifference and hostility to the project.

Asked what she thought public opinion to be, commissioner Premack responded: "I really don't know . . . If you pushed me against the wall I would say that people favored the Bloomington site. We spent a year and a half studying this thing," she added, "and I think we all felt that we knew a lot more than other people did."[34] "No, it had nothing to do with my decision,"[35] answered Kelly Gage. "The decision was based on facts presented," said Chairman Brutger. "We did what was right in our judgment."[36]

Why would the commissioners care about the public's opinion anyway? They were not electorally accountable to the people. They had two guidelines: the stadium legislation and their "best judgment." Undoubtedly commission members felt that they "knew a lot more" about the issue than other people did. Their decision would be "based on facts."

And the chosen seven had nearly a year and a half to collect these facts, over 500 days to mull them over, to scrutinize their every detail, and to reflect on their spiritual import. The commission was required to consider environmental impact statements, gather testimony from all interested parties and self-acclaimed experts, and assess public opinion through countless and long-winded hearings. No figure was left uncalculated. No opinion suppressed. After all, they were planning to build a sports stadium.

Or was it a fizzling rocket?

## The Neighborly Nobleman

Any community that wanted a stadium had to provide the land to the sports commission at no charge. Otherwise the commission could never meet the legislative bonding limits. The land in Bloomington was free. The land in Minneapolis was not. Although the 25-acre parcel was originally valued at $5.1 million, the price would be much higher. Most of the land was owned by Hennepin County and the Minneapolis Housing and Redevelopment Authority (HRA). The expenses involved in the land sale would not be limited to the parcel's market worth. The relocation of the County's Juvenile Center, for instance, would cost millions of dollars.

In July of 1977 John Cowles Jr. agreed to head the Chamber of Commerce task force to study ways to provide land for a Minneapolis stadium. Harvey MacKay served on the committee, as did many other leading business leaders including John Morrison, the board chairman of Northwestern National Bank; First National Bank chairman Dewalt Ankeny; Arley Bjella, chairman of the board of Lutheran Brotherhood, Kenneth Dayton, chairman of the board of Dayton-Hudson Corporation; and Chamber executive vice-president Charles Krusell.

Cowles' mission would be difficult. The land package might call for more than $10 million and possibly as much as $15 million in business pledges. Many Minneapolis businesses were already giving the five percent maximum of their pretax earnings to charities. The land ownership was complicated and the County Board was demanding a high price for both the juvenile center's land and its relocation costs. It was a deal that was going to take all of the ingenuity and business savvy that John Cowles Jr. could muster.

Cowles brought a touch of high-cultured intellect to a battle previously void of such refinement. A product of Exeter and Harvard, he learned the ropes of his father's newspaper business after graduating from college. He started out as a police reporter. In 1955 he shifted to the newspapers' publishing operations, serving as assistant business manager. Eventually John Cowles Sr. put the Star & Tribune in his son's care. Cowles also served as chairman of the board of Harper & Row and Harper's magazine, although the companies are no longer a part of the Cowles corporate collage.

John Cowles Jr. is the tissue and soul of corporate power in America. His words are carefully chosen. He shuns emotional speeches or impulsive postures. His mind works precisely. He dresses impeccably. He is an economic conservative and a social liberal.

Thus Cowles bears the outward trappings of corporate elitism. But the man's good works have shown another side. However weary it may sound, Cowles has a strong urge to civic duty, an almost obsessive desire to make a positive contribution to the community. He is one of the most generous givers to charity in Minneapolis. In the late sixties, he was an organizer of the urban coalition, a group of Minneapolis businessmen who served as "middle men" between discontented blacks and government agencies. It was Cowles who spearheaded the drive to build a theater for the Guthrie repertory company.

In the late fifties, renowned playwright Tyrone Guthrie announced that he was dissatisfied with New York's "wildly oversupplied, over competitive (Broadway) market." Five years later he surprised the theater world by moving his company to that bastion of prairie culture: Minneapolis. "It's hard to believe it now," said Cowles, "But nobody out here knew Tyrone Guthrie . . . it was all sort of a pipedream."[37]

After hearing that Guthrie was looking for a new home, Cowles set out to find a Minnesota organization willing to sponsor a theater. "The trick was I had to find an umbrella, a local partner to give the thing credibility."[38] He had no luck with the University, the Arts Institute, or the city of Minneapolis. Finally he got in touch with Harvey Arneson, who headed the University Arts Department and ran the Walker Arts Center. Arneson persuaded the Walker trustees to provide the land for the theater and contribute $300,000 towards its construction.

Cowles' next task was not an easy one: he had to collect millions of dollars worth of pledges from local businessmen. First he got a commitment from his father at the Star & Tribune. Secondly he solicited Atherton Bean of International Milling. Then he spoke with the Daytons. "And once they were in we were off to the races," he recalled. "It wasn't easy but we got the money . . . and when the plans came in for a million over budget we redesigned and did some more fundraising . . . we got the theater."[39]

And so it was with the stadium land. At first the task force estimated that they needed to collect between $5 and $10 million. They soon learned that it would be closer to $15 million. "We couldn't raise all of that money through charitable contributions," Cowles explained, "because Minneapolis companies likely to support the project were already giving their full 5 percent of pretax earnings or at least giving very generously to charities."[40] Rather than forcing these companies to choose between the stadium and the charities, the task force came up with the notion of forming a limited profit redevelopment company, the Industry Square Development Company (ISDC). Cowles referred to the company as a "public service investment" because earnings on its returns were limited to 6½ percent. The firm was "quite speculative — its main purpose was to make the stadium possible, not make money for us."[41]

In exchange for the purchase of the land for the stadium site and the allocation of $7.5 million to cover the county's expenses in relocating the juvenile center, the ISDC would get first rights to develop any land acquired by the Housing and Redevelopment Authority in the 25-acre Industry Square area. The company's rights applied only to the parcels of land the HRA owned or had on its acquisition list and not to the land directly needed for the stadium.

Charles Krusell, who was vice president of the development company under Cowles and later president, recommended the limited profit company to the task force. "We limited ourselves to the 6½ percent profit on investment in order to avoid criticism that we were involved for the money," he said. Krusell noted that the company's thirty stockholders would get less than half of the return they could earn from alternative investments. "We're in a partnership with the city," he said. "Because of our limited profit they might be the biggest beneficiaries. If a Faneuil Hall-type development occurred around the Old Milwaukee Depot [part of the 25-acre Industry Square site], for instance, it could produce large profits," noted Krusell. "The opportunity to make some money is there, but it really isn't going to benefit our limited profit corporation."[42]

A stadium and any surrounding development could very well increase the value of neighboring real estate, however. The Star & Tribune building was just a few blocks away from the proposed site. While the company's contribution would exceed any potential real estate benefits, a new stadium undoubtedly would enhance the value of the newspapers' land. "That's one of the reasons I felt the company should be among the leaders in putting cash into the project," explained Cowles, ". . . so that people wouldn't think we were backing a downtown stadium just in order to have the value of our real estate increase."[43]

On November 15, 1978, fifteen days before the commission was to make the site decision, Cowles announced that at least 42 business firms, including the Minnesota Vikings football team, had pledged $14,750,000 to pay the costs of the stadium land package. $10.7 million of the pledge came from private investors who promised to buy common stock in ISDC if Minneapolis was chosen as the stadium site. The remaining money — $4 million — was given in the form of tax deductible charitable contributions.

The Star & Tribune made the largest commitment — $4 million in cash and $900,000 in land (the company owned ¾ of a block of the Industry Square area). The First National Bank and the Northwestern National Bank each pledged $1 million. The Vikings agreed to commit $972,500 until other businesses could be found to pay for all or part of the remaining sum.[44]

The stadium commissioners now had two alternatives. They could either build a stadium on the land in Bloomington or sell that land and use the land in Minneapolis. It was time to get the calculators out. With less than two weeks left, stadium advocates on all sides were preparing for their last foray. Charts and estimates were fine. But there must be other ways to convince a commissioner.

### Final Testimony

"I was never lobbied by anybody...We were an arm's length from everyone. I knew in my case that if they had tried to lobby me it would have been counterproductive."[45]
— Dan Brutger

The Minneapolis and Bloomington lobbyists could try to sway the commissioners all they wanted at the public hearings, but individual lobbying was taboo. Admittedly there were some attempts at personal persuasion. "I know one of the commission members received a phone call from Max Winter pressuring him to go downtown and Harvey MacKay once offered to drive Gornick to the airport," remembered Solveig Premack. "But that was about the extent of it . . . And that's something most people don't believe."[46]

But the city and the suburb didn't need behind-closed-doors lobbying to plead their cases. They were championing their causes for all to hear. The Bloomington Stadium Committee took out a full-page advertisement in the Minneapolis papers entitled "Why a downtown stadium doesn't make sense." The ad, which ran two months before the final commission decision was due, showed a rickety domed stadium plopped in the middle of Minneapolis, surrounded by relentless smog, grossly entangled traffic, gas-masked tailgaters, and wild-eyed juvenile delinquents.

"If it's an economic decision, we can't lose," announced Bloomington Mayor James Lindau at one of the final hearings, "but if it's a political decision, we can't win."[47] The Mayor charged that Commissioner Premack did not qualify as an impartial judge of the issue because of her close ties to the Star & Tribune. Premack retorted that since her husband's death she had no interests, "financially or otherwise," in the paper.

Lindau acknowledged that the loss of the stadium would not cripple the suburb. "It [the stadium] does something for Bloomington," he testified, "it does something for our image." The Mayor also argued that the Bloomington parking lot, when used for tailgating, was an integral "part of the sports scene."[48]

Both cities were spending a lot of money to accommodate seven commissioners, all of whom stated emphatically that they would be swayed by "facts only." But if the commissioners could truly be persuaded by facts, then Minneapolis would provide them. The Minneapolis Chamber of Commerce and City Council split the cost of a $40,000 research survey to tell them (and the commission members) that a stadium constructed downtown would generate more construction, more taxes, more employment and less traffic than a stadium located in Bloomington. A downtown stadium would reduce travel distance, which would translate into gasoline savings to the tune of 425,000 gallons a year. The total driving and walking time to and from a downtown stadium for the average person would be 81 minutes, where as in Bloomington it would be 109 minutes. City Clerk Schwarzkopf argued that the minimal downtown parking was an advantage: the fans would be more dispersed in parking lots, easing the traffic after a game. There was better bus service downtown, making the stadium more accessible for people without cars.

In the closing months of the deliberations only one commissioner came forth with any indication as to his or her preference. "I'm for remodeling the Met and building a new football-soccer stadium," said commissioner Radman in August. "We have a helluva good baseball stadium in Bloomington."[49] Governor Perpich had been wrong about Radman's vote. The commissioner's allegiance to St. Paul and St. Paul labor clearly outweighed his ties to Dave Roe and the AFL-CIO. Radman warned that a domed stadium would cut into the business of the Metropolitan Sports Center (in Bloomington), the Minneapolis Auditorium, and the St. Paul Civic Center. "We don't need anything competing with them,"[50] he said.

Radman's public condemnation of a downtown dome triggered the previously silent Max Winter to come forth with some comments of his own. "My position is that we need a covered stadium for the Vikings with the weather problems we have here," he said in late August. "I don't care where it is. If they build an open stadium, the Twins and the Kicks can play in it if they want, but not the Vikings. We've got one of those now."[51]

To illustrate his point Winter flew out to meet with Bill Robertson, president of the Los Angeles Coliseum. The Rams were vacating the arena that year and Robertson was looking for new tenants. "This is not a scare tactic," argued Winter, "I went to Los Angeles only as an escape valve, to protect the

Vikings."[52]

By the last week in November the commissioners thought that everything that could have possibly been said about a stadium in Minnesota had been said, doubled, and compounded. The arguments aroused the same deja vu in Minnesota as "I Love Lucy" on television.

But on Nov. 22, 1978, the commissioners learned that there was one last catastrophe on the horizon. And it left them absolutely dazed. The message was straightforward: No dome, no Super Bowl. Vikings' General Manager Mike Lynn offered two new theses:

A. The absence of a dome hurt the Vikings' chances of signing draft choices by exposing them to the horrors of a Minnesota winter.

B. The lack of cover forced incumbent Vikings to practice away from home before championship games. These final practices coincided with the holiday season. And, according to Lynn, the players got homesick.

"Most of our players have young children and I saw team morale slip last year when we had to leave town early during the holidays," argued the general manager. "I find myself wondering if similar occurrences had anything to do with our losing four Super Bowls."[53]

"I'm a little disappointed the Vikings would blame the loss of four Super Bowls on the lack of a downtown stadium," responded Commissioner Gage. "Is it true," he continued, "that well-paid professional players can't spend four days away from their families without loss of efficiency?"

"It is a true fact,"[54] lamented Lynn.

The final blow has been struck. With this informational bombshell the commissioners adjourned.

"Thank God," sighed one observer, "that Calvin didn't testify."[55]

## The Jury's Verdict

On December 1, 1978, the Metropolitan Stadium Commission faced four options: it could build a multipurpose open-air stadium in Bloomington for football, baseball and soccer; it could remodel the Met and build an open-air football and soccer stadium in Bloomington; it could build a multipurpose domed stadium in Minneapolis; it could decide not to do anything. The fourth alternative had never been a very popular one. After 18 months of painstaking analysis, pages of statistics and estimates, reams of drawings and graphs, momentum had been building. "Doing nothing" would have signified a most anticlimactic end to the proceedings. The commissioners would have had nothing to create.

With the exception of Richard Radman, the chosen seven had been virtual paragons in their public statements. No one else had revealed a preference before the December meeting. Not even Jimmy the Greek attempted to call this one. "The commissioners made independent decisions," said Brutger. "Nobody knew until the final day which way the vote would go."[56]

The first to speak on December 1 was Josephine Nunn. She voted in favor of a domed stadium for Minneapolis. Then Richard Radman declared his "strong" support for the Bloomington site. He warned that a downtown dome would be too costly to complete. Radman quoted from St. Luke: "For which of you intending to build a tower, sitteth not down first, and counteth the cost, whether he have sufficient to finish it?" he read, "Lest haply, after he hath laid the foundation, and is not able to finish it, all that behold it begin to mock him, saying, this man began to build, and was not able to finish."[57]

Marion Kennon and Kelly Gage joined the labor leader in his support for the Bloomington site. Kennon questioned the use of energy to support a dome at a time when the nation was experiencing an energy crisis. "We are not dealing with sports teams anymore," declared Gage, "We are dealing with theater." He charged that indoor games would be mere television events. "If it is to be a television performance, let's do it on a sound stage."[58] In spite of the fact that the Vikings had sent a letter to each commissioner the day before the meeting informing them that it would be "exceedingly difficult" for the team to sign a long-term lease for an open-air Bloomington stadium, Gage believed they would.

Solveig Premack offered the view that building a domed stadium now would be better than refusing, having the teams leave, and then having to build one later to attract other teams. Her decision to vote for Minneapolis, however, was based mainly on economics. Because of the high water table in Bloomington, it would have been impossible to build a dome and more expensive to build an open-air stadium. Since the land provided by Minneapolis was free, money from the sale of the Bloomington land could be used to pay for the dome.

Chairman Brutger, who arrived at the meeting with a typed statement which he made available to each commission member, also supported the Minneapolis site. "In choosing the Minneapolis alternative," he wrote, "I am simply making my best judgment based on what I perceive to be in the long-term public interest." He agreed with Premack that it would be impossible to sign long term leases with the teams for an uncovered stadium. He felt that it was probably the last opportunity to secure a covered stadium with such limited public expenditure. According to Brutger, the University would benefit from a downtown covered stadium because of its close proximity to campus. The chairman also noted that Bloomington "may be the greatest beneficiary of a stadium in Minneapolis." A major development on the Met Stadium site "could produce substantial tax revenue and other benefits as early as 1983."

With a 3-3 tie Gornick would cast the deciding vote. Ronald Gornick had been the only commissioner to avoid stating his choice earlier in the meeting. Noting that the generations were changing — that his kids, who lived five blocks from an ice rink, insisted that he drive them to skating — Gornick asserted that Minnesota sports fans today needed a dome. Acknowledging that team preferences played an important role in his decision, Gornick cast his vote for Minneapolis.

The vote was a close one. But 4-3 or 7-0, the decision was binding. A stadium was to be built in Minneapolis.

For eight years the stadium controversy had been marked by unforseen obstacles, surprising twists, and painful bumps and bruises. Its December 1 conclusion was no different. After the decision had been handed down, Max Winter received several threats on his life. Donald Poss had a window shot out of his car. The stadium commission offices were evacuated because of a bomb threat. An unidentified man burst into their offices the following day and made threatening statements. He was removed by an armed guard.

The commissioners had endured dangerous voyages to unprotected Minnesota hinterlands. They had warded off the mischief and guile of lobbyists and braved the cannons of suspicious critics. Now they had survived threats on their very lives. But the fun wasn't over yet. They still had to build a stadium.

This was the Bloomington conception, in an ad that appeared in Twin City newspapers, of a stadium in downtown Minneapolis.

## Commissioners:

Josephine Nunn

Ronald Gornick

Kelton (Kelly) Gage

Dan J. Brutger

Marion C. Kennon

Richard C. Radman

Solveig Premack

108

**Donald Poss**

KEY

□ INDUSTRY SQUARE
RENEWAL AREA

■ ACQUISITION
PROPERTIES

The Industry Square investment by Minneapolis businessmen became a focal point of the stadium controversy.

3-15-76
Minneapolis Star and Tribune

"On a cold Sunday in December, which of you gentlemen wants to be the one to tell the Parkettes that they are going to have to travel all the way down to Industry Square to cheer on the Vikings?"

# Stadium Site Task Force
# Greater Minneapolis Chamber of Commerce

*Report on Investments and Contributions*
*February 1, 1982*

| Company | Investments in Industry Square Development Company | Contributions to Minneapolis Community Development Agency** | Contributions to Metropolitan Sports Facilities Commission | Total |
|---|---|---|---|---|
| Company | Investments in Industry Square Development Company | Contributions to Minneapolis Community Development Agency** | Contributions to Metropolitan Sports Facilities Commission | Total |
| Company | Investments in Industry Square Development Company | Contributions to Minneapolis Community Development Agency** | Contributions to Metropolitan Sports Facilities Commission | Total |
| Minneapolis Star & Tribune Company/Foundation | $ 3,307,000* | $ 1,418,000 | $ 412,000 | $ 5,137,000 |
| Dayton Hudson Foundation/ Corporation | 153,000* | 1,000,000 | 100,000 | 1,253,000 |
| First Bank Minneapolis/ Charitable Trust | 827,000* | | 100,000 | 927,000 |
| Northwestern National Bank of Minneapolis | 827,000* | | 100,000 | 927,000 |
| Honeywell, Inc. | 500,000 | | | 500,000 |
| Investors Diversified Services, Inc. | 500,000 | | | 500,000 |
| Carlson Companies, Inc./ Foundation | 65,000* | 300,000 | 100,000 | 465,000 |
| Lutheran Brotherhood | 296,000 | | 100,000 | 396,000 |
| The Pillsbury Company | 350,000 | | | 350,000 |
| Burlington Northern Railroad Company | 300,000 | | | 300,000 |
| Midwest Federal Savings and Loan Assn. | 100,000 | 200,000 | | 300,000 |
| Northwestern Bell Telephone Company | 300,000 | | | 300,000 |
| Midwest Radio-Television, Inc. | 250,000 | | | 250,000 |
| Northwestern National Life Insurance Company | 250,000 | | | 250,000 |

**This was the financial involvement of Minneapolis business in the Industry Square development program and the stadium.**

111

| | | | | |
|---|---|---|---|---|
| Graco Inc./Foundation | 150,000 | 50,000 | | 200,000 |
| Medtronic Inc. | 200,000 | | | 200,000 |
| Northern States Power Company | | 200,000 | | 200,000 |
| Prudential Insurance Company of America | 200,000 | | | 200,000 |
| International Multifoods | 150,000 | | | 150,000 |
| Minnesota Gas Company | 150,000 | | | 150,000 |
| National City Bank of Minneapolis | 150,000 | | | 150,000 |
| Twin City Federal Savings and Loan Association | 100,000 | 50,000 | | 150,000 |
| Dyco Petroleum Corporation | 125,000 | | | 125,000 |
| Gelco Corporation | 125,000 | | | 125,000 |
| Dahlberg Electronics, Inc. | 110,000 | | | 110,000 |
| Apache Corporation | 100,000 | | | 100,000 |
| Control Data Corporation | | | 100,000 | 100,000 |
| Jacobs Industries, Inc. | 100,000 | | | 100,000 |
| I.S. Joseph Inc. | 100,000 | | | 100,000 |
| Land O'Lakes, Inc. | 100,000 | | | 100,000 |
| M.A. Mortenson Company | 100,000 | | | 100,000 |
| Minnesota Vikings | | 100,000 | | 100,000 |
| North American Life and Casualty Company | 100,000 | | | 100,000 |
| Pepsi-Cola Bottling Company of Mpls./St. Paul | 100,000 | | | 100,000 |
| Riverside Industries | 100,000 | | | 100,000 |
| F & M Savings Bank of Minneapolis | | 75,000 | | 75,000 |
| Peavey Company | | 75,000 | | 75,000 |
| Ted Glasrud Associates | 65,000* | | | 65,000 |
| Alexander & Alexander of Minnesota, Inc. | 50,000 | | | 50,000 |
| Faegre & Benson | | 50,000 | | 50,000 |
| First Bank St. Paul | 50,000 | | | 50,000 |
| Marquette National Bank of Minneapolis | 50,000 | | | 50,000 |
| Phillips Foundation | | 50,000 | | 50,000 |
| Piper Jaffray & Hopwood Inc. | | 50,000 | | 50,000 |
| Tri-State Land Company | | 50,000 | | 50,000 |
| Munsingwear | | 45,000 | | 45,000 |
| Valspar Corporation | | 35,000 | | 35,000 |
| Rembrandt Enterprises, Inc. | | 32,500 | | 32,500 |
| Curtis Hotel | | 30,000 | | 30,000 |
| Erickson Petroleum Corporation | | 25,000 | | 25,000 |

| | | | |
|---|---|---|---|
| Groves Foundation | 25,000 | | 25,000 |
| Kensington Investments | 25,000 | | 25,000 |
| Mackay Envelope Company | 25,000 | | 25,000 |
| Midland National Bank of Minneapolis | 25,000 | | 25,000 |
| O'Connor & Hannan | 25,000 | | 25,000 |
| Tennant Foundation | 25,000 | | 25,000 |
| Jefferson Foundation | 22,500 | | 22,500 |
| Napco Industries, Inc. | 21,000 | | 21,000 |
| American Linen Supply Company | 20,000 | | 20,000 |
| MCM Industries, Inc. | 5,000 | | 5,000 |
| Johnson & Higgins | 4,000 | | 4,000 |
| Naegele Outdoor Advertising of the Twin Cities | 1,000 | | 1,000 |
| TOTAL | $10,500,000 | $ 4,059,000 | $ 1,012,000 | $15,571,000 |

**formerly Minneapolis Housing and Redevelopment Authority

*Investments in Industry Square Development Company include the following stand-by commitments:

| | |
|---|---|
| Minneapolis Star & Tribune Company/Foundation | $307,000 |
| Dayton Hudson Corporation/Foundation | 153,000 |
| First Bank Minneapolis/Charitable Trust | 77,000 |
| Northwestern National Bank of Minneapolis | 77,000 |
| Lutheran Brotherhood | 46,000 |
| Carlson Companies/Foundation | 15,000 |
| Ted Glasrud Associates, Inc. | 15,000 |
| | $690,000 |

**Other Major Participants in the Stadium Project:**

General Mills: Ticket purchase agreement with Vikings to avoid local television blackout: $1,500,000

Purchasers of the October 15, 1979, issue of Metropolitan Sports Facilities Commission-Metropolitan Council revenue bonds:

| | |
|---|---|
| Northwestern National Bank of Minneapolis | $20,000,000 |
| First Bank Minneapolis | 15,000,000 |
| First Bank St. Paul | 15,000,000 |
| St. Paul Companies | 5,000,000 |
| | $55,000,000 |

"Both Bloomington and Minneapolis really thought
that their stadium site was better for the public. So
we set aside our parochial differences and agreed on a
fair decision-making process. We would let an
unbiased group make the decision. The best site
would win."[1] — Senator Steve Keefe.

# 6

# THE DELEGATES DECIDE

The citizen commission's 1978 decision to bu'' a domed stadium
in the city of Minneapolis was made by only seven individuals.
While the commissioners were not oblivious to the wishes of
interest groups, they were not particularly receptive to their
demands. They did not have to be. Thus the commission's
decision cannot be explained by patterns of influence. Instead it
was determined by the motivations, values, and personal biases
of seven citizens. Each commissioner had a unique perception of
his or her role and responsibilities, each held a particular view as
to what constituted the public's interest.

The Metropolitan Stadium Commission was created by the
Minnesota legislature. The commissioners were required to obey
the stadium law. They had to follow each and every mandate.
The lawmakers could dissolve the commission if they wished.
They could remove its bonding authority or cut off its funds by
repealing the liquor tax. Legally, the commission was dependent
on the state government. But in actuality it was "fiercely
independent."[2] Its December 1 decision was insulated from the

direct control of democratic politics. The commissioners were accountable to no one — not the legislators, not the interest groups, not the people.

The commission represents a phenomenon of American politics that began soon after the New Deal: the transfer of authority from the legislative branch of the government to the bureaucratic one, the creation, in effect, of another branch of government. Because of the openness of the American political process, because of the proliferation of interests, decisions are almost never made quickly. Sometimes they are never made at all. There is a tension between the nature of the political system and the requirements of coordinated policies and consistent planning. Thus political matters are often removed from the realm of politics; delegated to political appointees; handed down to bureaucrats, independent boards, and citizens' commissions. Here, it is thought, issues will be settled efficiently and competently, without the political "dirty work," without the interest group hassling.

There is a certain appeal to this "apolitical" mode of decision-making. Things seem cleaner, neater. Decisions are more comprehensive and prompt. In the hands of the commissioners, the stadium issue was no longer considered a legislative beachball to be tossed to and fro by prevailing political winds. Rather it was a "business challenge," requiring the commissioners' "organizational and creative abilities."[3] The seven members were "neutral judges," citizen jurors who would be fair and just.

But the commissioners were also appointed deputies. They came from designated geographic areas and sympathized with different interest groups. They had differing views of their roles. Some considered themselves to be "citizen jurors." Others were "interest advocates." These conflicting conceptions, along with individual values and perceptions, help to explain the final outcome.

## Decision-Makers as "Citizen Jurors"

The commission's deliberations were heralded as a "fair decision-making process." The group's decision would be "unbiased." It would be made by citizens as opposed to politicians. "The best site" would win. To reinforce this "unbiased" decision-making, the Governor chose people who had not previously participated in the controversy, citizens who had not expressed an opinion on the issue. The majority of the commissioners were, prior to the appointment, totally uninformed on the issue. Solveig Premack, for instance, had never even attended a Twins' or a Vikings' game. She was not only neutral on a stadium, but had little personal interest in retaining the teams.

The citizens were far from stadium experts when they were chosen. "None of us knew a thing about stadiums,"[4] noted executive director Poss. The commissioners approached stadium building openly and inquisitively. Just as uninformed jury members reach a verdict after hearing testimony and examining the evidence, they learned the ins and outs of stadium construction through their travels and public hearings. After 18 months of training, the seven citizens became experts on the issue. They felt that they "knew a lot more than other people did."[5] While public opinion may have been an important consideration to legislators, it was of little consequence to the commissioners. They would decide "on the basis of facts"[6] and their own conceptions of what constituted the public's interest.

The commission's appeal rested upon the assumption that it was possible and desirable for a group of competent and "disinterested" people to decide what outcome would best serve the public's interest. Because of their good will and accumulated knowledge, these people could decide which alternative would be "best for all."

There are two problems with this assumption. First of all, it requires that the personal values and public interest conceptions of one individual, or a small group of individuals, take priority over those of the public at-large. Secondly, it is practically impossible to find a person void of personal biases and preconceptions which would influence his decision on any particular issue.

"There is likely to be a systematic bias in a technician's choice of value premises," writes Edward Banfield. "He will ignore or underrate those elements of a situation that are controversial or not conventionally defined; he will favor those that can be measured, especially those that can be measured in money terms.''[7] Many of the commissioners, or stadium "technicians," seemed to favor tangible, "measurable" data over intangible claims that could not be "conventionally defined." Solveig Premack was asked if she considered the positive impact the stadium might have on the central city — the jobs it might provide for low income people and the advantages of having construction take place in the city as opposed to the suburb. "That wasn't really an important consideration," she said. "I made my decision on the basis of economics."[8] Public opinion did not weigh heavily in the commissioners' decisions. It was "hard to define . . . it was always changing."[9] The concerns voiced by "Save the Met" (that ballgames should be played outdoors), and the Bloomington Mayor's argument that the stadium was important to the city's image, could not be measured in dollar terms. The Minneapolis land gift, on the other hand, which allowed the Commission to both build a stadium and sell the Bloomington land, could be measured economically. Decisions based on "hard facts" minimize and underrate intangible considerations. While it makes sense that the commissioners would be attracted by arguments grounded in numbers and facts, it does not necessarily make them more important.

It is quite obvious that the commissioners were not entirely "neutral" or "apolitical." One cannot rid oneself of past preconceptions or present biases. Nor can one disregard future repercussions. Richard Radman had been a St. Paul labor leader before the decision; he would be a St. Paul labor leader after the decision. Kelly Gage admitted that he had a "bias toward Bloomington" because it was "more accessible"[10] for the people from his area. Ronald Gornick had an allegiance to the governor. The commission as a whole held a bias toward constructing a new stadium, whether it be domed or undomed. Like any group, it was concerned with enhancing and maintaining its own influence. If it chose to build nothing, the commission would have still existed to operate a remodeled Met, but with considerably less prestige and sense of accomplishment.

While the majority of the commissioners made an honest attempt to be open-minded, they were not altruistic angels. But perhaps they were not supposed to be. "Perpich was as fair as a person could be when he picked the commission," said Bloomington legislator Benedict. "Geographically, it was representative, and he tried to balance off as many interests as he possibly could."[11] Each of the seven members was chosen to represent a certain area or group. Yet it was literally impossible for a commissioner to be both a "citizen juror" and an "interest advocate." These two conceptions, were, for the most part, irreconcilable.

## Decision-Makers as "Interest Advocates"

Simply because someone lives in a certain area or belongs to a certain race or religion does not imply that he or she will act to further that interest. Exemplifying an interest is not equivalent to advocating it. There is a vast difference between descriptive representation and substantive representation. Descriptive representation requires that a group of individuals should be microcosm of the population at-large. The group's composition is a mirror image of the people it represents. Substantive representation, on the other hand, is defined by a person's actions. It requires that the individual's behavior is intended to benefit the interests of his or her constituency.

Governor Perpich did his best to make the commission descriptively representative. But generally the commissioners did not substantively represent the conflicting interests involved in the stadium controversy. Although polling results were sketchy, it seemed that most outstate residents preferred that no new stadium be built. Yet all three outstate commisisoners voted in favor of a new stadium (2 for Minneapolis, 1 for Bloomington). It also appeared that many Minneapolis residents were hostile to the idea of a stadium in their city. Minneapolis representative Solveig Premack voted in favor of the Minneapolis site. The majority of St. Paul and south suburban residents definitely favored a Bloomington site. The representatives from the two areas — Radman and Kennon — voted on line with these groups. Josephine Nunn, who represented the northern suburbs, voted in favor of the Minneapolis stadium. North suburban residents were more supportive of the Minneapolis stadium than southern suburbanites: Minneapolis was closer to their homes than Bloomington.

The commissioners' responsiveness to their home precincts should not be confused with the responsiveness of elected representatives. Unlike political officeholders, the commissioners did not have a stake in the outcome. While a politician might be defeated in re-election if she disregarded the interests of her contituents, the commissioners would not be kicked off the commission if they failed to "represent" their area (as could very well be the case with a politician). The stadium legislation did not insist that the appointees should be responsive to their geographic areas. Each of the commissioners treated the appointment differently. Commissioner Gage spoke of the "people from my part of the state."[12] Radman noted that "we don't want anything competing"[13] with the St. Paul Civic Center and other area arenas. Premack, on the other hand, remarked, "I was independent . . . There's not really much they could have done to me."[14]

Critics of the Minneapolis stadium argued that the commission process had been fixed; that the final outcome had been "in the cards" since the members' appointments. Governor Perpich acknowledged that he and his staff members considered how the appointees would vote. One would expect that they thought about it. Perpich knew three of the commission members. He had worked with Gage and Premack. He was a friend of Gornick's. If he implicitly exercised influence with any of the commissioners it was Gornick. "He knew what I wanted," noted Perpich, and "that might have been enough."[15]

But the Governor seemed to be more concerned with getting the issue out of the Capitol and appointing a "fair" and "broadly representative" commission than he was with influencing its outcome. Rudy Perpich had an election approaching. He did not wish to be accused of "stacking" the commission. He had never been overly enthusiastic about the project in the first place. It was Anderson's baby. Perpich never contacted the commission members during the decision process. Over the months of deliberations, they developed a "strong sense of independence."[16] They "kept an arm's length"[17] from everyone.

The commission's final decision was a mixture of individual motivations, values, and opinions. Some members approached the decision as a "citizen juror." Others perceived themselves as "interest advocates." At least one member, Ronald Gornick, may have felt obligated to the man who appointed him. Each person's decision hinged in part upon his or her estimate of the relative importance of competing values. Was it more important to preserve football and baseball as outdoor sports or to make absolutely certain that the teams remained in the area? Did the economic and social needs of the city of Minneapolis take priority over the needs of the city of St. Paul and Bloomington? The decisions also depended on the individual interpretations of the facts: Could a Minneapolis stadium be built within budget? Would it benefit the University of Minnesota? Would it lead to more energy consumption, because of the energy needed to inflate and heat the stadium? Would it lead to less energy consumption because of gasoline savings?

This analysis has not attempted to determine precisely what factors were most important to each commissioner's decision. While one can postulate and theorize as the commissioners' reasoning, it is impossible to document each individual choice. The lesson to be learned from the commission's decision is more general, however. When a problem is hammered out through the political process, the criterion for decision is the distribution of influence. A controversy's outcome is determined by the relative amount of influence exercised by each conflicting interest. But when the problem is taken out of the political arena, when authority is delegated to a small number of people who are not electorally accountable to the public, the criteria used to reach a decision are personal ones. The decision-maker places the problem in the context of his or her own values, preconceptions, and future goals. "In choosing the Minneapolis alternative," noted Chairman Brutger, "I am simply making my best judgment based on what I perceive to be in the long-term public interest."[18]

The stadium commissioners were responsible and thoughtful, efficient and well-meaning.

But they did not have to face the voters.

The delegation of authority from elected representatives to non-elected appointees poses an obvious danger to American democracy today. Bureaucracies and independent boards were created to facilitate democratic decision-making, to ease the passage of projects and policies through laggard and meandering legislatures. But as more and more decisions are made by "panels of experts" and "citizens commissions," the control of decision-making drifts farther and farther away from the political office-holders — and from the people who elect them.

The Metrodome won no high awards for architectural aesthetics. But it opened on time and under budget.

3-17-76
Minneapolis Star and Tribune

"The possibility that a downtown stadium might be a burden on the
taxpayers seems to have the administration in Bloomington worried sick."

> "The people correctly perceive that their tax money is being used to make the rich richer. John Doe is paying for the stadium and he can't afford to go to the games."[1] — Senate Majority Leader Nick Coleman

# 7

# THE STADIUM: 1979-1982

On May 11, 1977, the Minnesota legislature decreed that an impartial citizens' commission would determine the design and location of a new stadium. Legislators from all over the state, including lawmakers from Minneapolis, Bloomington, and St. Paul, agreed to accept the commission's decision as binding. On December 1, 1978, after 18 months of deliberation, the commission chose to build a domed stadium in Minneapolis. Minnesotans breathed a sigh of relief. Once and for all, the eight-year controversy was settled. It had been decided fairly, without the political horsetrading, without the legislative dramatics. Everyone was glad to bid the implacable stadium issue a long-overdue farewell.

Just a moment, not everyone.

In January of 1979, Representative Ray Faricy and Senator John Chenoweth, both Democrats from St. Paul, introduced companion House and Senate bills to repeal the 2% metropolitan liquor tax enacted to guarantee bond repayment on the arena. If the tax were repealed, there would be no bond sale, and without the bond sale, there would be no stadium. Two years earlier, John Lifteau, a bar owner from Afton, a town on the metropolitan area's eastern outreaches, challenged the tax in county court. Lifteau claimed that the tax was unconstitutional because it served no public purpose. A district judge ruled in favor of the bar owner because parts of three cities which were split by the metropolitan borders were exempted from the tax. The Minnesota Supreme Court overturned the lower court's decision, however, and ruled that the tax was legal.

The tax, it was advertised, would provide "backup" revenues for bonds only until 1980. But one provision of the stadium law apparently allowed the commission to use the tax money for the arena's operation if it chose to build a domed stadium. Stadium officials estimated that the dome would require the continued collection of the liquor tax at least into 1985. "We thought that the liquor tax was a backup tax to ensure the sale of the bonds," declared an incensed Senator Chenoweth in a committee hearing. "It has become an outright subsidy." According to Chenoweth, the legislators were not told that the tax would be used to pay for operating costs on a stadium. "There are enough holes in that proposal to drive a Mack truck through,"[2] he charged.

"I bitterly resent the implication that we tried to mislead the legislators in this matter," retorted Minneapolis Senator Steve Keefe, one of the sponsors of the 1977 "no-site" bill. Keefe played a two-year-old tape of his testimony in which he had detailed the domed stadium tax provision. According to Keefe and other Minneapolis stadium advocates, the purported confusion over the tax was nothing more than a rallying cry for sore losers. "During the 1978 session there was not one murmur about the backup tax," remembered Charles Krussell, "and it was being collected the whole time."[3]

While the seven-member stadium commission took the position that they would not become involved in the tax repeal issue, one member, Ronald Gornick, had some spicy words for the legislators. "Speaking as an individual," Gornick remarked that members of the commission were paid only $50 a meeting, "and those clowns at the legislature, who are getting $15 or $20 thousand a year, say we haven't done the job . . . They didn't want to decide the site," reflected the commissioner, "but now some of them are unhappy with the decision and they're using the tax issue as a cover for their real objections."[4]

The problem was not the tax. The problem was that the stadium commission had chosen a site. "As soon as they lost," noted Senator Keefe, "you knew they would poke their noses into it and try to screw it up."[5] But "they" were not a single, unified group with a common set of objections to the tax. "They" came in many shapes and sizes.

There were, of course, the legislators from Bloomington and St. Paul who objected to the Minneapolis site decision and resented the fact that bar drinkers from their areas were being taxed for a Minneapolis project. For starters, Representative Ray Pleasant of Bloomington drafted a bill less than two months after the commission's decision to shift the stadium site to Bloomington. Two senators who had helped to engineer the "no-site" bill through the legislature in 1977 — St. Paul Democrat Coleman and Richfield Republican Kirchner — tried a more subtle approach. They backed Chenoweth's tax repeal bill. Calling his support for the 1977 bill and associated tax "the most unpopular thing I've done in my district in sixteen years in office," Coleman proposed that the 2 percent metropolitan liquor tax be repealed and replaced by a tax on Minneapolis commercial property. "We just didn't foresee the emotional furor it would create among bar drinkers,"[6] bemoaned the St. Paul Democrat.

Perhaps it wasn't the St. Paul bar drinkers who opposed the tax as much as it was the St. Paul bar owners. They did not want to charge their customers an extra 2 percent on every drink to pay for a Minneapolis stadium which would eventually benefit their competition across the river. These bar owners, along with a sprinkling of their patrons, organized a protest group set on repealing the tax. They called themselves "COST" — Citizens Opposed to the Stadium Tax. Fred Primoli, owner of Primo's Food and Liquors, was chairman. Primoli, who hired an extra bartender so that he could devote more time to the organization, remarked, "I know what the 2 percent means to the people who patronize my place. They're paying 75 cents for a highball that would cost them 70 cents . . . and they're people to whom a nickle means something."[7]

In January of 1979 COST staged a protest march from the St. Paul cathedral to the Capitol. What the group lacked in numbers (there were barely 150), they made up for in spirit. A passionate allegiance to the cause was a prerequisite for anyone who chose to trudge through drifted snow in 8 below zero temperatures. Members of "Save the Met", a group of young outdoor sports enthusiasts organized during the commission hearings, marched alongside the St. Paul bar contingency. "All I'm trying to do is save the aura of American sports, save the aura of fun,"[8] said Julian Empson, head of "Save the Met."

People from both groups, along with neighborhood activists from Elliot Park and Cedar Riverside (the two neighborhoods bordering the proposed stadium) combined forces to form "MADD" — Minnesotans Against the Downtown Dome. Approximately twenty MADD members made daily pilgrimages to the Capitol during the winter of 1979. They also marched and sang in front of the Star & Tribune building, criticizing the newspaper and its owner, John Cowles Jr., for alleged slanted news coverage on the stadium issue. MADD member Brian Coyle, who likened the stadium protest to the anti-war uprising of the sixties, described his view of the stadium situation: "Here you are, trying to build your own community. Suddenly outside forces with enormous resources and power try to build this vast project — ironically underwritten with public money."[9]

Coyle wasn't the only stadium opponent hostile to the project because of the involvement of the Minneapolis business interests. Democratic legislators resented the fact that some Minneapolis stadium promoters had contributed to Republican campaigns in the past November election. "It was Rudy Perpich who gave them a downtown stadium" jeered one bitter senator, "and all the time they (the Minneapolis businessmen) were lined up to knife him in the back."[10]

The 1978 elections provoked an unprecedented turnover in Minnesota politics, ending an era of Democratic dominance at both the state and national levels. The once popular Governor Wendell Anderson, who had resigned to fill Walter Mondale's vacant senate seat, was defeated by Rudy Boschwitz, a self-made millionaire and flamboyant plywood manufacturer. Anderson's decision to appoint himself to the senate seat did not enthrall Minnesota voters, nor did his waffling stands on many of the campaign issues. The State's other senate seat, also up for election in 1978 because of the death of Hubert Humphrey, was captured by a little-known moderate Republican, David Durenberger. He outdistanced maverick Democrat Robert Short, a sports financier and hotel tycoon who spent millions of dollars to finance his campaign. Earlier Short had defeated the endorsed Democratic candidate, Donald Fraser,[11] in a bitter primary. Durenberger, like Boschwitz, had never previously held an elected office.

For the Democrats, the results were as bleak at the state level as they were at the national level. Governor Rudy Perpich, the affable miner's son who had been elevated from lieutenant governor to succeed Wendell Anderson, lost narrowly to Republican Congressman Al Quie. Several Democratic incumbents lost their seats in the state House and Senate elections. Of those who did retain their offices, many were just narrowly elected.

In an election marked by a high degree of voter discontent with Democratic policies and leaders (a forerunner of the 1980 presidential election), the stadium issue was hardly the primary impetus for the local Democrats' defeats. In a scattering of cases — particularly those involving St. Paul and Minneapolis incumbents who had voted in favor of the "no-site" bill — it might have turned some votes. But the commission didn't choose the Minneapolis site until after the election. In spite of the fact that the tax repeal proponents liked to use the incumbents' defeats as a rallying cry during legislative debates, the issue was not a major one in the election.

But those Democrats who had been re-elected were bitter about the defeat of their friends and colleagues. They particularly annoyed with the Minneapolis businessmen who had aided the Republicans to victory. Six members of the Minneapolis Chamber of Commerce gave a total of $11,250 to Governor Quie's campaign, including a $5,500 campaign contribution from John Cowles Jr. "The D.F.L. is the victim of a big snow job . . . We got blasted," proclaimed Minneapolis Democrat Eugene Stokowski at a meeting of stadium supporters. Stokowski suspected that the Minneapolis *Star & Tribune* and owner Cowles were partly responsible for the tax repeal backlash. "Your (newspapers') attacks on Wendy Anderson were in the paper day after day," he charged, pointing a finger at Cowles. "And what about the other Senate job you did on Bob Short and Don Fraser? . . . The mood of the election has put this project in jeopardy and you aren't innocent."[12]

If John Cowles Jr. should have been held responsible for putting anything in jeopardy, it was not the stadium project but the credibility of his newspapers. His editors and columnists supported both sides of the stadium issue and, contrary to what many believed, Cowles had nothing to do with the content of the papers' news stories and editorials. But readers were cynical about the papers' supposed neutrality in reporting the issue. "It wasn't the newspaper who supported the stadium," explained Cowles, "it was me and the company." "My distance from the actual reporting and editing of the news was great. There were layers and layers of people between me and the news."[13]

According to one reporter, Cowles should not have expected the average reader to "make a distinction between the corporation and the editors."[14] The Star ran several editorials criticizing its owner's active role in the stadium controversy. "It is safe to say we don't agree on the role of the corporate executive in community affairs,"[15] said the Star's editor, Steve Isaacs. Cowles' involvement prompted 45 Tribune staff members to place an ad in their paper's March 1 issue. "Our role is to report, not to participate in, these issues," they wrote. "We bought this advertisement to assure readers that our professional principles have not been undermined by Cowles' involvement in the stadium issue."

The papers' editorials and the reporters' affirmation of neutrality on the issue failed to convince the members of MADD, however. The group registered a complaint with the Minnesota Press Council alleging that the two papers had slanted their coverage in such a way so as to "promote the construction of a downtown stadium."[16] MADD members felt that Cowles' ownership of the paper was an invaluable resource, allowing him to exercise undue influence in the stadium battle. According to MADD leader Brian Coyle, the stadium battle typified "fights against heavy-handed brokers wheeling and dealing with other peoples' lives, whether they sit in the Pentagon or the Minneapolis Chamber of Commerce. To me, the stadium is a domestic Vietnam War."[17]

Another pro-tax repeal group did not share Coyle's emotional objections against the stadium project. They were the rural legislators. Their hostility toward the liquor tax had little to do with resentment against John Cowles Jr. and the Minneapolis power structure, or even with the tax itself (their constituents did not live in the metropolitan area). Rather they were opposed to the project because the commmission had chosen the Minneapolis site. Many of these legislators had originally voted for the no-site bill only because they felt the commission would opt for a Bloomington stadium. "If Bloomington had been the site," said one rural representative, "we wouldn't have such strong sentiment on the liquor tax issue."[18] According to Clarence Purfeerst, a Democratic Senator from the southern Minnesota town of Faribault, people in his district were opposed to the downtown stadium. Purfeerst had voted in favor of the "no-site" bill two years ago. Now he would vote to repeal the liquor tax, "If it were in Bloomington," he noted, "there would be no objection."[19]

"Remember that 40 percent of those who voted for the stadium last session are back in their fields and business offices,"[20] cautioned Senator Ed Schrom before the vote on the Senate repeal bill. The senators heeded Schrom's warning. On Feb. 8, they approved the stadium tax repeal by a 38 to 27 vote. Twelve senators who originally voted for the 1977 stadium law voted to repeal the tax. Of those twelve, ten were from outstate districts. Even the former Governor's brother, Senator George Perpich of Chisholm, rescinded his 1977 support for the stadium. He said the liquor tax amounted to "welfare for the wealthy."[21]

Now the action shifted to the House. Unexpectedly, stadium advocate Roe announced that organized labor would no longer support the project because the legislature had not been paying enough attention to labor interests. Roe wanted to get the repeal measure to a Senate-House conference where it could be used to gain concessions on labor legislation. The project's sudden lack of labor support did turn some house members' votes in a key committee, and, according to Roe, it prompted legislators to act on other labor issues. But the conference committee was unsuccessful. On April 2 the House voted to repeal the liquor tax, 71 to 63.

On April 9 Governor Quie announced that he would sign the repeal bill. The commission's decision was no longer meaningful. Without the tax, it was impossible to sell the bonds to build the stadium. The state government had waved its magic wand. The Minneapolis stadium had vanished. "Now we can start over again,"[22] noted the Republican governor.

Was the new governor serious? Were the legislators destined to debate the stadium once more? To find a new site? To come up with a new design?

It appeared that Governor Quie was dead serious. He even suggested a new site — the University of Minnesota. According to University officials, the renovation of the 50-year-old Memorial stadium would most likely cost more than building a new stadium in Minneapolis. What is it they say? Old stadiums never die . . . they only get remodeled . . .

## The 55 Million Dollar Question

> "We viewed the 1977 stadium bill as a contract between our club and the legislature. They were to build a stadium. We were to play in it. You don't break a contract without future repercussions."[23]      — Mike Lynn

For years Mike Lynn had kept his NFL comrades up-to-date on the status of the Vikings' efforts to secure a new home. At the league meeting in March of 1979, the general manager had some unpleasant news: the Minnesota legislature was going to repeal the stadium tax. According to Lynn, the league owners were sympathetic with the Vikings' plight. While previously they were not receptive to a Vikings' move, "If we had asked for a vote of approval in March of 1979 we would have gotten permission to leave," said Lynn. "If the legislature did not approve a stadium bill in 1979 we would have most definitely called a special meeting of the league and asked for permission to move."[24]

Many of the legislators voting in favor of the repeal claimed that their vote was inconsequential because the teams would have never signed the 30-year leases in the first place. "They wanted us to take the blame," explained Lynn, "but we threw it back into their laps."[25] Lynn met with the commission and ironed out the principal terms of the lease. Although Calvin Griffith refused to attend the meeting, they communicated with him by phone. The teams prepared a joint press release which stated that they had agreed to the main terms of the lease.

While the press release was not equivalent to a binding contract, it demonstrated that the teams were willing to commit themselves to expensive rental agreements for the right to play in a bigger and better Minnesota stadium. And the new governor and legislature feared that the Vikings and Twins might actually leave town if they were not provided with that bigger and better Minnesota stadium. The legislative session ended May 21. The lawmakers had less than two months to come up with an alternative plan. The legislative leaders initially explored the possibility of remodeling Memorial stadium. The University Board of Regents voted unanimously to endorse the concept if the remodeling provided space for intramural sports and physical education. This proposal lost some of its appeal, however, when University officials estimated the project's cost at $63 million.

Next Senate leaders introduced a bill for an open-air Minneapolis stadium. The bill limited costs to $46 million and provided that Minneapolis commercial property, liquor, and hotel-motel taxes be collected to back the bond sale. The plan evoked fiery responses from the Vikings' management and the Minneapolis business community. Lynn warned that the Vikings' tentative agreement for a 30-year lease was not automatically transferable to an undomed stadium. Chamber executive director Krusell declared that the $14.5 million worth of land contracts with commerical donors and investors all specified a "domed stadium." "It's my view that the land would not be available for an uncovered stadium, at least as far as the business community is concerned," cautioned Krusell. "There's not much interest in an open stadium among our members."[26]

"It sounds like the chamber is trying to challenge us to a game of 'chicken,' " retorted Senator Nick Coleman. "You know, that's the one where two people get into two cars and drive straight at each other at a high speed and see who turns away first," he explained. "If they want to play that way, O.K."[27]

But many legislators felt that losing the teams would be more troublesome than losing face in a confrontation with the Minneapolis businessmen. In April Mike. Lynn met with House and Senate majority leaders and "told them a number of things."[28] In a letter to the legislators, Lynn warned that the team would most likely leave without a new stadium. Lynn's efforts paid off. By the end of April the Senate approved a new stadium financial package by 43 to 22. The bill took the commission's Minneapolis site decision as binding. It authorized a hotel-motel and liquor-by-the-drink tax restricted to the city of Minneapolis.

On May 20, the bill, amended in conference committee, came to a vote before the House. The representatives voted in favor of the proposal, 66 to 65, two votes short of the 68 needed to pass. One of the primary reasons the bill failed to receive enough support was a provision inserted in the conference committee. It restricted the use of state highway funds to roads built "solely" to give access to a new Minneapolis stadium. Some rural legislators feared that Minneapolis officials would argue that no road was built "solely" for the stadium. Thus the provision would enable them to use more state funds for Minneapolis roadwork. "You don't fool around with the highway fund and expect to get rural votes,"[29] remarked one representative.

One day later the bill appeared again. The word "solely" had been deleted from the roadwork provision. Governor Al Quie and House speaker Rod Searle had spent the preceding 24 hours pressuring legislators who had voted against the new tax to change their minds. "We're back to the same old ballgame," scoffed stadium opponent Jim Swanson.

"Mr. Swanson," speaker Searle cooly replied, "There will be no ballgame without a stadium."[30]

By a vote of 72 to 59 the representatives approved the Minneapolis hotel-motel and liquor tax. The governor signed the new bill. But the stadium proposal had one more stopover. Ironically, it returned to the chambers where it had originated nearly a decade before — the Minneapolis City Council. The council had to approve the 2 percent liquor tax and the 2.5-3 percent hotel-motel tax (the exact amount would be determined by expenses) before the commission could authorize the bond sale. By a 9 to 4 vote, the council approved the tax increase. Mayor Albert Hofstede fully endorsed the project.

The city's hotel-motel industry already carried a 3 percent city tax and a 4 percent general sales tax. Yet nine owners and managers of major Minneapolis hotels sent letters to aldermen voicing their support for the tax. They felt the stadium would generate enough business to compensate for the tax increase. One hotel owner who did not send his warm regards was Robert Short of the Leamington Hotel. Short, who had been defeated in his quest for public office six months before, was also a sports team financier. He had owned both the Minneapolis Lakers basketball team and the Washington Senators, later the Texas Rangers, baseball team. Yet Short had little gratitude or sympathy to spare for either the sports industry or the public. He suggested spending $50 million of state funds which were already earmarked for income and property tax relief to pay for the stadium. "Don't give that tax to me," he declared in a press conference. "If you do, you'd better believe we'll wind up in court."[31]

Short wasn't the only one to threaten legal action. The issue had been argued over in every barroom from Beaver Bay to Ortonville, debated in every conference room from the Vikings' offices to the State Capitol. It was only fitting that it should eventually emerge in an even loftier setting: the courtroom. And after the teams had negotiated the leases, it seemed like everyone had a law suit.

## Who Will Sell the Popcorn?

"The Minnesota Twins have the worst-managed business organization I've ever seen. They come to meetings unprepared, and then they leave for golf!"      — Don Poss

While the Vikings and Twins had tentatively agreed to the stadium leases in April, the agreements had not been officially contracted. State law required that both teams sign the 30-year lease agreements before the bonds could be sold. Since interest rates were increasing and the legislation specified that the stadium bond interest could not exceed 7 ½ percent, the sooner the bonds could be sold, the better. If the lease negotiations took too long there was a good chance the bonds would not be sold at all.

"My attitude was that if we couldn't negotiate team leases that were going to allow us to follow the stadium law, then the Vikings and Twins were going to have to leave," recalled Don Poss. "They knew that I meant it and they knew that Dan (Brutger) meant it . . . We weren't going to subvert the intent of the legislation in order to keep them here."[32]

One conflict emerged early in 1979. The Minnesota stadium law required that television blackouts of local games be lifted when 90 percent of the stadium seats were sold 72 hours ahead of the game. The NFL required the team to sellout 100 percent of the seats before the blackout could be lifted at the Met, in keeping with league policy. The 90 percent sellout requirement, which would improve the odds of televising local games, directly conflicted with the NFL policy. In January of 1979, owners of 26 of the 28 NFL teams voted against allowing the Vikings to operate under the legislation's 90 percent blackout provision. They were worried that legislatures in other states would pass similar laws.

Unless the discrepancy between the state law and football league requirement could be eliminated, the Vikings could not play in a new stadium. The problem was settled when General Mills, a Minneapolis-based corporation, offered to act as a "donor," and buy up the remaining seats when fewer than 10 percent were left unsold three days before the game. Thus both the legal and league requirements could be met.

In July the commission reached a lease agreement with the Vikings. The team was to pay 9½ percent of its after-tax ticket receipts as stadium rent in addition to the 10 percent stadium ticket tax. Thus the stadium rent from the Vikings would total 19½ percent of ticket revenue. The Twins would pay a total of 17½ percent of their ticket revenue. The teams' rent money would be used to pay off both the bonds and the operating costs. According to Poss, the Vikings and Twins agreed to two of the highest stadium rents in the nation.

But the Twins' lease was not nearly as easy to negotiate as the Vikings'. With their attendance slipping yearly, the baseball team claimed that they could not afford to sacrifice the concession rights they owned at the Met. The commission insisted that they would control the food and drink sales so that a good part of the concession revenues would funnel back into the stadium.

The Twins' spokesmen also claimed that they could not afford to pay for new office space. While many professional stadium commissions provide office space for teams, the Minnesota legislation did not allow for such frivolities. If the teams wanted office space or spectator boxes, they would have to build them themselves. The Vikings chose to construct their own business offices and practice facility in suburban Eden Prairie. The Twins requested office space at the new stadium.

After weeks of commission bargaining with Calvin Griffith's son Clark, nephew Bruce Haynes, and Twins' lawyer Peter Dorsey, the negotiations had reached an impasse. The team still wanted to retain its concession rights and have the commission pay for their offices. In early August chairman Brutger began daily one-to-one meetings with Calvin Griffith. "As much as Calvin loves them (his family), he doesn't trust them with his business," noted one commission source, "until we got Calvin involved it was just shadow play, not the real thing."[33]

Griffith's mom-and-pop organization and parsimony have been cited as reasons for the team's demise in the past decade. "The Minnesota Twins are the worst-managed business organization I've ever seen," said Don Poss. "They come to meetings unprepared, and then they leave for golf dates . . . they're a throwback to the feudal age."[34]

Calvin Griffith has a propensity for surrendering key players to his competitors, lacking the money — or the willingness — to match the big-buck bidders. But if Griffith was a miser with his players, he was even more stingy at the stadium negotiating table. Calvin wouldn't budge.

After weeks of frustrating negotiating, Brutger and Griffith finally reached an agreement. While the commission's original intent was to write parallel leases for the teams, Griffith managed to wangle some major concessions out of the commissioners. While he did not receive the full concession rights he demanded, the Twins' owner was allowed 30 percent of gross concession receipts until the team's attendance reached 1.4 million. After this point, the Twins would receive 20 percent. The Vikings, on the other hand, were limited to 10 percent of concession revenues.

The lease also contained an escape clause which allowed the baseball team to ask to be released from the contract if its attendance fell below 1.4 million in each of three consecutive seasons or if it experienced net operating losses in three successive years. While stadium architects maintained that the dome's design would make air-conditioning unnecessary, the Twins were worried that the lack of cool air would cut into their attendance. Thus another provision was added to the lease: if the team could prove that attendance was slipping because of the summer heat, they were not bound to play at the metrodome if the commission refused to install air-conditioning. Finally, Griffith was determined not to sign the lease unless he was reimbursed for the office space the team would lose at the Met. The baseball owner would pay no more than $700,000 of the 1.7 million needed to build the team's offices in the new stadium.

Fearing that the stadium bond sale would be irreparably delayed because of Griffith's obstinance, John Cowles Jr. and members of the Minneapolis Chamber Task Force stepped in and offered to donate the $1 million to the commission for the Twin's office space.

Somehow, some way, the Twins' "bumbling" baseball owner, whose organization had been characterized by one stadium negotiator as a medieval relic, had wheedled $1 million out of the city's top legal and financial impresarios. The business chieftains would pay for Cal Griffith's office space.

## A Call on Sunday

"We didn't think we were writing an allegory," declared Senator Nick Coleman after the Twins' lease had been signed. "We thought we were writing a statute."[35] Coleman was outraged by the commission's concessions to the baseball team, particularly the team's three-year "escape clause." He was also ranting over the one percent discrepancy in the fee charged by the Twin Cities investment banking firm, Piper, Jaffray, and Hopwood, that was commissioned to sell the bonds. The legislation specified a .9 percent bonding fee, and the company was charging 1.9 percent. "The commission is making wildly liberal interpretations of the stadium legislation,"[36] he charged. Before the bonds could be sold, Coleman was going to take the commission to court.

Whatever motivated the Senate majority leader to contest the commission was not clear. In the past Coleman had vacillated on the issue. He had alternately championed the no-site bill, the tax repeal bill, and the Minneapolis tax bill. Perhaps the Senate's senior member wanted to kill the stadium, or gain favor with his St. Paul constituents, or assure that the commission's actions were legal. Maybe, as one newspaper editorialist suggested, Coleman "simply wanted to have the last word."[37]

Whatever his reasons, the St. Paul Democrat was able to find some noteworthy allies. Defeated Senate candidate Bob Short (who had previously threatened to sue over the hotel-motel tax), and Senate Minority leader and long-time stadium opponent Robert Ashbach joined Coleman in his suit against the commission's interpretation of the stadium law. "Why should we support Max Winter and Calvin Griffith," asked Ashbach, "If we subsidize them, why don't we subsidize Munsingwear, Articat and beauty parlors?"[38] While each of the three plaintiffs had a different reason for involving himself in the suit, they shared a common purpose: to delay action on the stadium. The more they could stall the bond sale, the bleaker the chances would be to find buyers. Already in September the venture was speculative. While other revenue bonds across the country were being sold at interest rates of 8½ or 9 percent, the Minnesota law limited the stadium bonds to a 7½ percent maximum interest rate.

Coleman, Short, and Ashbach (nicknamed the "unholy trio" by their critics) weren't alone in their efforts to thwart the bond sale. Law professor Jack Davies was another antagonist. Davies was a Democratic state senator from Minneapolis who had opposed the project from the start. "Jack Davies is different from most of the other stadium opponents," contended Senator Keefe. "He has a fundamental, philosophical objection to public subsidies for private industries." Keefe also noted that Davies was from a district where opposition to the stadium was useful politically. "His timing with the anti-stadium efforts usually coincided with primary fights with left-wing opponents . . . He's the senior person in the senate and he never has an easy election . . . Every year they think he's going to lose and somehow he manages to pull it off."[39]

One lazy summer afternoon in 1979 Jack Davies was sitting out on his back porch catching up on some "light summer reading." The law professor was perusing the Minnesota statute books. Davies discovered an obscure provision in the state's constitution which specifies that any state law which applies to a *single unit* of government — such as the city of Minneapolis — can be modified by an amendment to the city charter. The liquor and hotel-motel tax law change, which applied only to the city of Minneapolis, made the state law a special law applying specifically to the city. Davies asked that a charter amendment proposing cancellation of the taxes be placed on the citizens' ballot.

"I don't believe in referendum government," he acknowledged, "so it was something of an embarrassment that I was fighting against initiative and referendum at the same time I was pushing this stadium tax referendum . . . But I wanted a vote on that charter amendment."[40] Davies gathered the necessary 7,700 signatures (5 percent of the electorate) to force a charter amendment vote. He hoped it would be placed on the November 6 ballot. The senator's amendment was not introduced in time to be placed on the ballot. Nevertheless, Davies was sure that the potential illegality of the tax scheme would discourage prospective bond buyers. "I thought that once I had started that charter petition the lawyers would tell the buyers that it would not be safe to buy the bonds," said Davies, "and it almost worked . . . at least it knocked them off the national market . . . but then the local banks popped."[41]

By the second week of October the bonds remained unsold. At this point Don Poss gave up hope. It was simply too late. The sale was a month overdue. In September the bond purchase would have "represented a reasonable, acceptable investment."[42] But not in October. Interest rates were rising dramatically. The Coleman-Ashbach-Short law suit and Davies charter amendment drive had stalled the bond sale. The bonds were "unattractive on the national market."[43] Officials from Piper, Jaffray, and Hopwood decided to offer the bonds locally, to Twin Cities financial institutions. While the local private-sale approach cuts selling costs, it is usually not used because it requires the payment of an interest bonus as an inducement to investors. An interest bonus was impossible, however, because of the legislation's limited-interest rate. But since there was support among business leaders for the project, the investment bankers hoped that the Twin Cities banks and financiers would buy the bonds without the interest bonus.

On Friday, October 12, Don Poss left the commission offices convinced that the stadium would not be built. Poss was prepared to "come into work on Monday and begin studying the rehabilitation of Met stadium." But then on Sunday morning the stadium director received a telephone call from the Minneapolis stadium boosters. They wanted him and chairman Brutger to come in and talk with the potential bond buyers. "Well the whole power structure was there," Poss said, "the businessmen, the bank representatives . . . and the deal was made . . . on a Sunday, of all days."[44] The institutions that bought the bonds — First National Bank of Minneapolis, First National Bank of St.

Paul, Northwestern National Bank of Minneapolis, and the St. Paul Companies — appeared to be motivated more out of a sense of civic duty than a chance for future profit. "They could have used their money for better gains somewhere else," noted Poss. "As far as I'm concerned, they made a civic contribution on behalf of their shareholders."[45]

The bonds were sold. The stadium law was upheld in court and the "unholy trio" declined to appeal their law suit. Jack Davies, however, would not give up on his suit. He eventually brought the constitutional complaint to the State Supreme Court. The case was heard in 1982, after the stadium had already been built. "When Jack gets a cause under his skin," explained Kelly Gage, "he really isn't deterred by what most people see as . . . practicalities . . ."[46]

## To Build a Stadium

"We didn't have to hire a law firm or an architect that we didn't want. We didn't owe anyone favors. We didn't have to hire cronies...we ran the commission like you'd run a business."[47]     — Dan Brutger

There were not many people who believed that the stadium commission could actually build a domed stadium for under $55 million. Other stadium officials across the country were certainly doubtful. The politicians were skeptical. Even most of the stadium promoters were not convinced that it was possible. Construction on the project began in the fall of 1979. The Metrodome was scheduled to be finished by April of 1982 — just in time for the Twins' opening game.

In April of 1982 the project was completed.

It was built more than $8 million under budget.

In a time when both private and public constructions incur millions of dollars in cost overruns, when "projected expenses" skyrocket because of inflation and unexpected delays, when government agencies are infamous for careless budgeting and frivolous spending, the Metrodome's net savings was stupendous. "People always ask me how we did it," mused Chairman Brutger, "and I tell them we did it by commitment . . . we said we *will not* spend any more money than the budget allows. From day one we imposed that on everyone who worked on the project," said Brutger, "the architects, the staff, the designers, the engineers . . . everyone. We would not be one cent over budget."[48]

By encouraging competitive bidding, the commission was able to cut millions from the estimated contract costs. It kept a close eye on the bidding by personally letting the primary contracts and by hiring a construction management firm to solicit, supervise, and evaluate bids. "There wasn't a board or nail going into the structure without the construction management firm knowing what it would cost," recalled Solveig Premack. "We broke everything into small bid packages so that people knew exactly what was expected of them . . . they couldn't pad the contracts."[49] Hiring a large number of small firms also enabled the commissioners to contract out to more minority-owned firms — 5 times as many as the legislation specified.

Brutger's construction savvy and Poss' hard-skinned managerial style were evident every step of the way. According to Brutger, the commission saved millions of dollars by double checking the plans. If the commission had stuck with the architects' suggestion to use stainless steel knuckles on the 52 stadium supports, for instance, it would have added major and unnecessary expenses to the construction costs. The use of the less expensive steel knuckles did not detract from the building's aesthetic or structural value, and it saved $250,000. The construction managers also discovered that designers had erred in their choice of concrete finish. A change from the original class of finish, which according to Brutger, would have made the stadium corridor floors "smooth enough for an atomic bomb laboratory,"[50] saved the commission $750,000.

In addition to the competitive contracting and meticulous construction managing, a breakthrough in stadium design not only helped the commission save money, but also improved the stadium's sight lines. Rather than starting with a larger circular design in order to accommodate a baseball field, the commission began with a smaller, oval stadium for football. The circular structure, used in most multipurpose stadiums, requires the addition of seats for football and soccer. The Metrodome's smaller football field, on the other hand, can be enlarged into a baseball field by collapsing 5,700 seats, in the same manner as a high school gym. The design is less expensive because it calls for less volume. The Metrodome also has better sight lines for football and soccer than any other multipurpose stadium.

The commissioners were lucky to catch a dip in the construction business. Construction firms were hungry for work at the time and were willing to turn in low bids. "But even without this economic factor," noted Brutger, "the stadium would not have gone over budget. You also have to remember that the $55 million limit was set in 1977 and the stadium was completed in 1982," he said. "If you figure in inflation, we were over $30 million under budget."[51]

While the construction costs of the stadium were limited to $55 million, the non-construction costs — the architect, managment, and equipment fees — were not included in this figure. The total cost is estimated at $72 million. But the only part of the total which was financed by bonds was the construction. The remaining costs were paid by contributions and the interest earned on the bonds. The hotel-motel and liquor tax, which produces approximately $2½ to $3 million in revenues each year, will be "phased out sooner than people think," remarked director Poss, "probably before 1983."[52]

The Met stadium land, which had been appraised at $5 to $7 million, was sold for over $18 million because of the highly competitive bidding. With interest, the stadium commission should collect over $25 million from the land sale. The high-priced sale will also benefit Bloomington. Former Senator Benedict predicted that the tax revenue generated from the stadium land's commercial development, will be a "financial bonanza"[53] for the suburb.

The commission savings were used to pay back the bondholders at a faster rate than was expected. The extra money also allowed the commissioners to install seats instead of the originally planned contour benches, glaze the finishes of the public concourses, and plant more trees around the arena. They used approximately $3½ million of the budget surplus to install their own concessions. Instead of allowing a private concessionaire to reap the food and drink profits, they hired a "concessionaire consultant." The commission would own the concession rights and control the production and profits; the concessionaire would manage the business for a flat rate. This arrangement, which had been successful in Anaheim stadium, allows the stadium authority more flexibility and higher profit potential than conventional concession agreements.

According to Don Poss, it is perfectly conceivable that, after the bonding institutions have been reimbursed, the stadium could make a profit. "But that's something we don't want to do . . . if we were in the private sector, we could do that," said Poss. "But as long as we keep putting the money back into the stadium we're o.k." "We might be independent of politics," he acknowledged, "but we're a public agency just the same."[54]

## Final Rumblings

"If we were your typical bumbling government bureaucracy, a year behind schedule with huge cost overruns, everyone would feel sorry for us. Oh they'd write about it and have fun with it...but they'd feel sorry for us. But we were successful. And now everyone is grumbling that we rooked them."[55]                     — Don Poss

One would assume that the commission's economizing would have inspired hearty applause from all corners of the stadium ring. But in a story that has consistently eluded happy endings, it is only appropriate that the saga's final chapter should be punctuated by further unrest and rebellion. If there was money to spare, there were plenty of people who felt they deserved it.

The city of Minneapolis requested the use of $2 million of the commission's budget surplus for relocating the city streets and installing water and sewer lines.

"Absolutely not," responded the commissioners. The stadium law forbids the use of bond proceeds for anything but stadium construction.

The Minnesota Vikings had a request. They wanted the commission to annul the 10 percent ticket tax. "I ask Poss how much money he has in the bank and he won't tell me," complained Lynn. "They don't need the 10 percent ticket tax . . . it's a joke."[56] Lynn tried to persuade legislators to introduce a law which would rescind the tax.

"Impossible!" balked the stadium commission. Not even legislators can violate a legal contract. The people who bought the bonds have a legal contract that the 10 percent ticket price will be in effect as long as the stadium is there. "If they'd pass a bill to rescind the tax," said Poss, "we'd take it to court and get it overturned."[57]

The Twins were another disgruntled claimant. They sued the commission for the $700,000 they paid for office space. If the commission was $8 million under, why should the Twins, who were operating in the red anyways, have to pay $700,000 for office space?

"Because you said you would," retorted the commission. According to Poss, the team's suit will never hold up in court. The payment was not contingent on whether or not the project was within budget.

The Twins weren't the only ones grumbling about office space money. The Minneapolis businessmen who pledged to pay $1 million for the Twins' office space asked that the debt be forgiven. "Dan Brutger convinced us that the whole thing was going to collapse unless we came up with an additional million for the Twins,' said John Cowles Jr. "But when we found out that they had a large surplus we said 'you don't need our money anymore.' " According to Cowles, most of the money was already earmarked for charities. "It wasn't going back to some corporate treasury,"[58] he said. But the stadium commission threatened to sue the business contributors for the million dollars and they had little choice but to acquiese. Their commitment, like the Twins', was not contingent on the project's deficit or surplus. According to Cowles, the commission's stubborness cooled the relations between the stadium commission and the businessmen's task force. "I think we will be less likely to respond to other things the commission might like us to do to help,"[59] noted Cowles.

"We are so damned independent that they'd like to hang us,"[60] reflected Poss. The Minneapolis people will not have to go to these extremes to replace the contentious commissioners, however. The 1979 hotel-motel and liquor tax statute gave the city the power to appoint six of the seven commission members by January of 1985. Only the commission chairman will be from an outstate area and appointed by the governor. Since Minneapolis accepted the tax burden, Minneapolis should have the right to control the commission. Donald Poss disagrees with this logic, however. He doesn't want to relinquish his position to a city bureaucrat. A suburban legislator, who by no small coincidence represented Brooklyn Center, the suburb where Poss had been city manager, introduced a bill to keep the existing geographic distribution of the commission. The bill was defeated in the 1982 legislative session. By 1985 Minneapolis will control 6 of the 7 commission memberships. These members will be able to appoint their own executive director. While Poss was a remarkable builder and manager, his increasingly combative attitude toward the city government and businesses has alienated him from these groups. Don Poss' days as a stadium director seem numbered.

Poss' frictions with his former allies were just one part of the 11th hour turmoil preceding the stadium's formal debut. The Minneapolis *Star* published a five page expose in October of 1981 entitled "The Dome Deal: Land, Power, and the Dome." The article detailed how "the city of Minneapolis signed over exclusive development control of the land around the downtown domed stadium to two consortiums of large Minnesota businesses without public scrutiny or discussion."[61] The thrust of the story was that at least five of the limited profit investors — among them John Cowles Jr. — put themselves in a position to avoid the 6.5 percent profit limitation when they turned some of their Industry Square development rights over to "City Venture," a private redevelopment organization. Five of the Industry Square stockholders also had holdings in the company. City Venture had acquired the rights to 15 of the 50 city blocks in the Industry

Square renewal area and was not limited to 6.5 percent profits.

But it was also acknowledged that City Venture, a national development company, had six months earlier dropped its plans to develop in the area. Its rights had reverted to ISDC. It was no longer possible for the joint stockholders to avoid the 6½% profit limitation. Cowles called the reported scam "a theoretical loophole that frankly had not occurred to us at the time we made the City Venture deal." He added: "The limits to man's capacity for suspicion are boundless."[62]

The "Dome Deal" story "would have been stopped if the subject had not been the stadium, City Venture and John Cowles Jr.," wrote executive editor Tim McGuire. McGuire, who believes that Cowles should not lead community projects because his "civic activism" puts his "journalists in a compromised position," nevertheless noted that "not a newspaper owner in the country has tolerated more criticism by his own newspapers or of the things he's associated with than John Cowles Jr." McGuire urged readers to understand that the expose was published "not in spite of John Cowles Jr. involvement in City Venture but because of that involvement."[63]

These are not the final rumblings to resound in the aftermath of the stadium project. There undoubtedly will be more criticism from the press, continued surveillance from the politicians, and additional soundings from the project's friends and enemies. When the political process remains open to such scrutiny, the people retain a hold on its outcomes. They may disagree with some of the policies and decisions which result from this process. The government's elected caretakers will sometimes fall short of their expectations. But when the process is sensitive and adaptable, when it is open to change, then its government will not be insulated from the people's control. This is what defines democracy. And this, in part, is how democracy serves the public interest.

The Metrodome defied the predictions — and the passions — of its critics by opening for baseball on schedule in 1982. Fans later complained about the lack of air conditioning, but the stadium managers said they would install it in 1983.

Members of the Minneapolis Tribune news staff bought an ad in their newspaper at the height of the stadium debate in 1979 to make clear they were not influenced professionally by the involvement of president John Cowles, Jr. in the dome.

"There is a drinking tax in force that was earmarked to pay for a covered sports stadium that has already been completed." page 290 "The new 80,000-seat metro-politian stadium in Bloomington..." page 289
United States 1979, a tour guide

GUINDON
Minneapolis
Tribune

12-10-78
Minneapolis Star and Tribune

"The decision was made in the legislature. They had created the commission to build a stadium. That was our charge. If they wanted to reverse it that was their right. But we had to obey the law. We had to implement it."[1] — Kelly Gage

# 8

# FROM THE CAPITOL TO THE COGWHEELS

The Twins' concessions arrangement and the commission's choice of concrete finish appear minute and tedious details when set against the stadium's larger political scenario. But these seemingly unimportant elements — the way the bonds were sold, the content of the teams' leases, the structure's design — told a story all their own. Together they shaped the way the stadium legislation was implemented. The problems encountered by the commissioners — the liquor tax repeal, the law suits, the difficulties in negotiating the leases and selling the bonds — illuminate the complexities of implementation.

It is the act of carrying out, of achieving ends. After the commission had chosen the stadium site (a decision which, in itself, was an implementation of the stadium law), it was faced with the arduous task of carrying out the provisions of the stadium bill. The legislative mandates were links in a chain of implementation. Every agreement was dependent on the next. First the project required a backup bond tax. The commissioners could not sell the bonds without it. Even with the tax, they could not implement the bond sale before they had negotiated the team leases. They were unable to begin the construction before they had sold the bonds. In order to attain the bill's final objectives — to build the stadium under budget and in accordance with the environmental, legal, and technical details of the legislation — they had to closely monitor the project's construction.

This is not the most captivating aspect of the political process. It lives on the nitty-gritty details and the small technicalities. Those who implement policy usually operate outside of the public limelight, their work carrying significantly less prestige than the jobs of those who make policy. But its outcome, the measure of whether or not the policymakers' objectives were attained, can literally make or break a public project.

The Minneapolis stadium legislation was implemented succesfully because the law which guided it was clear and precise. The people charged with doing it were capable and enthusiastic. The politicians who scrutinized it were watchful and demanding. In this way the story was unique. Usually the implementation of public projects and policies is not so visible, not so politically volatile. In most cases it is performed in a bureaucratic cocoon, the decisions are insulated from public consideration. Nevertheless, the commission's handling of the stadium project illustrates two general principles which can be applied to any project: the complexity and the art of implementing.

## The Political Obstacle Course

In their study of the implementation of a federally funded employment program in Oakland during the early seventies, Jeffrey Pressman and Aaron Wildavsky found "what seemed to be a simple program turned out to be a very complex one, involving numerous participants, a long and tortuous path of decision-making points."[2] Members of the Minneapolis stadium commission would certainly agree with that conclusion. While the legislative objectives seemed straightforward enough, the bill's implementation was not so easy.

A month after they chose the stadium site, the commissioners were confronted by the first of many disagreements and delays in the project's construction: the liquor tax repeal effort. While the tax repeal movement may have been heralded as "democracy in action," as a prime example of the people expressing their will by rejecting an unjust and unwanted tax, it is best understood as a natural consequence of problems resulting from implementation. "As soon as they lost," noted one senator, "you knew that they would try to screw it up."[3]

The site decision was the commission's first opportunity to implement the stadium law. When the decision was made, problems immediately arose. "If Bloomington had been the site," remarked one rural representative, "we wouldn't have had such strong sentiment on the liquor tax issue."[4] While some senators were angry with the site decision, others resented the Minneapolis businessmen's contributions to Republican campaigns in the 1978 election. Others feared their constituents' reaction to a "pro-stadium" vote. Whatever the reasoning, the apolitical aura of the 1977 no-site bill quickly faded after the site decision had been made. As Pressman and Wildavsky found in Oakland, "the apparent solidity of original aims and understandings gave way as people, organizations, and circumstances changed."[5]

The Minneapolis tax placed the burden on those who were most likely to benefit from the city's stadium. This seemed logical enough. But the origins of the repeal conflict were not to be found in the legislators' concern with the "fairness" of the tax. This concern, as commissioner Gornick noted, was "a cover" for the legislators' "real objections."[6] The bill had to be renegotiated because the circumstances — the site decision and election results — had changed. Many of the lawmakers were unhappy with the bill in its original form.

The stadium law, with its many requirements and specifications, provided endless opportunities for delaying the project. If a settlement had not been reached on the blackout law, for instance, or if the businessmen had refused to provide the $1 million for the Twins' office space, the chances that the stadium could have been built under budget, or, for that matter, built at all, would have been reduced. The attempted lawsuits demonstrate how delay can thwart the implementation process.

Because the stadium issue remained publicly visible throughout its implementation, it provided a spotlight for those politicians who chose to remain involved. Since there was such a multitude of participants, and numerous decision points where they could intervene, the project's risk of delay was particulary high. "When a program is characterized by so many contradictory criteria, antagonistic relationships among participants, and a high level of uncertainty about even the possibility of success," wrote Pressman and Wildavsky, "it is not hard to predict or to explain the failure of the effort to reach its goals."[7] Why then, was the stadium a success?

## A Different Kind of Art

Policymaking has been referred to as an "art." So has political argument and legislative strategy. Implementing them is most often considered a drudgery. "Conceiving" and "discussing" take precedence over "enacting" and "executing." Yet even the most well-meaning policies and carefully-conceived programs have been dashed by the hard realities of implementation. Sometimes the objectives are plausible, but those charged with implementing them are either unable or unwilling to administrate effectively.

Many felt that the expectations of the stadium legislation — to build a domed stadium for under $55 million — were too high. But those whose job it was to make the legislation work did not. Perhaps this is the primary reason why the project was successful. Poss, Brutger, and the other commission members had both the ability and the commitment to do it. The stadium project's high visibility gave their job more "stardom," more prestige, than a bureaucrat might reasonably expect in building a highway bridge, for example. The fact that the commission had in effect "made policy" by choosing the site, inevitably made it feel responsible for the project. The members had a genuine interest and stake in its outcome.

So the commissioners themselves, with their confidence and commitment, their emphasis on efficiency and careful planning, shaped the project's success. Their diversity was also an attribute. They were not sports enthusiasts or experts on stadium construction. The fact that the commissioners were not "jocks" gave them no qualms about being strong-willed in lease negotiations with the teams. The process of learning about stadiums made them open-minded to new construction ideas.

Putting tough business techniques into the commission made it something leaner and shrewder than just one more bureaucracy. The commission would never have saved so much money had it not encouraged competitive bidding on both the construction contracts and the Bloomington land sale. The decision to hire a management firm to monitor the building's construction was also cost-efficient. The notion of owning the concessions was another example of business profit-making incorporated into the workings of a public commission.

The commission's success, however, teaches more than the virtues of efficient stadium construction. The commission's experience is a model in the art of doing — the art of legislative implementation. The stadium bill provided a steady guide for the project's execution. It was both specific and demanding. And if the commissioners had any trouble following its mandate, the politicians, who continued to scrutinize the process, were sure to let them know.

"No government is more powerful than one whose agencies have good laws to implement," writes Theodore Lowi in *The End of Liberalism,* "nothing serves better to direct bureaucracy than issuing it clear orders along with powers."[8] When the discretion afforded to those who execute the laws is limited by strong and well-stated laws, when standards are set high, but expectations are attainable, a project's implementation stands a better chance of success. Laws must be geared to the demands of implementing them. For in the end, the true measure of a project's success is not the manner in which it was debated or the amount of time put into its conception. Its measure is the harmony between original intent and final outcome.

The Humphrey Metrodome was hailed by its supporters as a capital improvement that would help revitalize downtown Minneapolis. Despite the football strike, its early performance tended to support those claims. Predicted traffic snarls were practically non-existent. But it still generated little love among people who preferred baseball under sun — and football in sleet.

156

# CONCLUSION

Did the construction of the Minneapolis Metrodome serve the public interest? Some will say it most certainly did not. A domed stadium, they claim, turns sports games into theater. The teams are no longer playing football and baseball, but domeball, a climate-controlled, Orwellian version of sports in which the grounds-crew works with vacuum cleaners and the players stay spotless from opening kickoff to postgame interview.

Others will argue that the stadium represents a misuse of public funds and therefore conflicts with the public's interest. To be sure the stadium was not financed directly with tax money. But the time and energy public officials expended on the issue and the money generated from the liquor and hotel-motel tax would, in this view, be better spent on a project of greater social value than a sports stadium.

Its supporters believe that the Metrodome will benefit the community both economically and socially. The stadium will enlarge the tax base and increase jobs, creating a greater "economic ripple" than would a suburban stadium. Former city council president Louis DeMars maintains "It's the traffic of people coming downtown that's important. A lot of people are afraid to go downtown. They think that there are gangsters and hoods and strange folks downtown. If they come to watch the Twins and the Vikings they will be more apt to visit again."[1] This enhanced social welfare is one conception of how the project serves the public interest. Although former Mayor Naftalin regards football as a "barbaric sport," he maintains the stadium will serve the public interest because it will give the elderly and poor better access to ballgames, particularly Twins' games. "If they are going to gather to watch a game, then they should gather in the city. It is the city that needs the employment and the public exposure."[2]

All of these arguments appropriately bear on the Metrodome's relationship to the public interest. They appeal to normative values that exemplify certain conceptions of what will benefit the larger community. A democracy cannot flourish without the public airings of these values. It in itself is a system grounded in values such as "equal treatment" and "popular control." But to assert that the public is served because normative standards are met does not require a claim that individual wants are satisfied. In other words, equating the "public interest" with certain higher conceptions — conceptions that are not necessarily equivalent to the aggregate sum of individual interests — may subordinate the expressed opinion of the people. Thus, in addition to evaluating a government action by normative criteria, one should see whether it coincides with the actual preferences of individuals in a community.

Who is a better judge of what a person wants than the person herself? This criterion of the public interest, which judges an issue according to the opinions held by members of the general public, seems the most sensible way to determine whether a government's action serves the public interest. Polls provided the only evidence with which to assess public opinions on the stadium issue. Since the results of polling data hinge on the way questions are phrased and since people have little incentive to represent their true preferences, the polls should not be construed as the definitive measure of public opinion. But when they produce fairly consistent results — as was the case in the Minnesota stadium issue — their data is more creditable.

Throughout the seventies not one public opinion poll showed that either Minnesota, metropolitan, or Minneapolis residents favored a Minneapolis stadium over a Bloomington stadium — whether it be a new construction or a remodeled Met. As the struggle wore on, Met Stadium became imbued with a charm and quaintness — some of it inspired by the Bloomington lobby but much of it sincerely felt by the public — that gave the downtown stadium the appearance of an unwanted intruder. To the very end of the battle and beyond, when it was under construction and secure as an accomplished fact, the downtown dome had scant friends among the general public and even less among the ticket-buying clientele at the Met.

Many people automatically opposed the project because they assumed that if they supported it, they would have to pay for it. It was difficult for them to believe that the teams would actually leave the area if a new stadium were not built. Many of the legislators who debated the issue and devoted substantially more time to it than members of the public, on the other hand, were convinced that the teams would leave. Although the public may not have shared this fear, the legislators concluded that if a stadium were not built, and if one or both of the teams consequently abandoned the area, voters would have held it against them in the next election. Because the legislators were well aware of their constituents' concern with the stadium's cost, they would only agree to a financing plan which would not be a burden to taxpayers.

The claim is not that these politicians possessed some kind of higher knowledge that made them more capable of discerning the people's will than the people themselves. Another explanation for the discrepancy between the wishes of the public and the actions of their representatives is not so disturbing: Citizens cannot possibly be well-informed on every issue. They do not have the time or incentives to consider legislative issues in great detail. The people's delegates are not necessarily any more qualified or smarter or altruistic than the citizens they represent. But many of them spend a good part of their lives collecting the facts, weighing the issues, and making legislative decisions. It is their job.

While government "by the people" is theoretically desirable, because of the complicated and time-consuming nature of today's political questions, the government cannot consult the public on every issue. Sometimes government actions will diverge from the opinions polls reveal. But this does not necessarily mean the government's decision runs counter to the public's interest. With accountability there is a defense against evaluating public decisions as mirrors of popular opinion. The public will retain the "final word" on the actions of their representatives. "You can throw them out of office or not throw them out of office depending on how they perform," noted the city council president. "That's how democracy serves the public interest."[3]

This notion of evaluating the public interest as a reflection of individual wants both before and after a government decision has been made calls attention to the procedure used to reach a decision. If the people have access to the process, if conflicting interests are voiced, and an issue is debated in good faith, then the outcome of the process will presumably be closer to the public's interest than if it had been settled in a less open manner. This is the procedural conception of the public interest. It questions how a government copes with clashing interests and how it decides between them. It considers the justifications for government action, the way conflicting demands are articulated and balanced, the manner in which an issue is resolved and the decision implemented.

The study of the Minneapolis Metrodome has attempted to evaluate the public interest in this way. It followed a project through the workings of a city government, a state legislature, and an independent commission. At each stage questions were raised as to whether the decision-makers' actions served the public interest. Perhaps the greatest defect of the Minnesota government's handling of the stadium issue was that the conflict over the project's location was resolved by an independent commission not accountable to the people. The commission, nevertheless, was controlled by a demanding and detailed bill created by elected representatives. The issue was generally aired in good faith. It was certainly afforded considerable deliberation. From the time the stadium was first debated in the city council, to the time it opened its gates to baseball fans, it was subject to careful public scrutiny.

Viewed as a reflection of public opinion, the Minneapolis Metrodome is an uncertain example of a government serving the public's interest. Seen as the resultant of a fair political process, the government's balancing of diverse wants stands as an arguably good example of how the political process serves the public interest.

There will always be disagreements over whether a project as emotionally charged as the Metrodome benefits the public. But there can be a general agreement as to whether the process used to reach that decision is in the public interest. If the public constrains and ultimately controls its delegates' decisions, then its interest is imbedded in every outcome. This is a view of the public interest that is not limited to a single issue. It is the lifeblood of politics.

# EPILOGUE, 1986

In 1982, when the Metrodome first opened its gates to baseball fans, the project was heralded as an economic success. The Minneapolis Dome, which was built primarily with private funds, came in under budget and on time. Its proponents claimed that this was only the beginning. A new stadium, they said, would be a catalyst for downtown development, and it would boost game attendance and the city's somewhat stagnant night life. Eventually, they predicted, the Dome would be economically viable, no longer in need of support from the public coffers.

Now, four years later, we can gauge the extent to which these predictions have held true. First, it is important to note that the Twins and the Vikings are still playing ball in Minnesota. Unlike Oakland, which lost its Raiders to Los Angeles, and Baltimore, whose Colts recently bolted to Indianapolis, the Twin Cities have held onto their teams.

Economically the stadium has been quite successful. Both the liquor and hotel-motel taxes were lifted in 1984. With the exception of the indirect state subsidy in the form of real estate tax exemptions, the Dome is basically self-supporting. Although optimistic stadium promoters forecast an economic boom for the area surrounding the dome, the stadium has failed to generate any sizable development.

Game attendance has been strong, with the exception of baseball games scheduled on sunny weekend afternoons. The Commission's remedy for this? The Twins now try to schedule all Saturday games for the evenings. Fears of snarled post-game traffic and nonexistent parking have been largely allayed. According to Jerry Bell, the present Executive Director of the Stadium Commission, the Vikings' attendance is always good and the Twins' attendance has nearly doubled since the team moved into the Dome. And while there have been a few sparks of hope for the Twins' success during their four seasons of Domeball, the boosted attendance can hardly be attributed to a vastly improved winning record.

In addition to the Twins and the Vikings, the stadium hosts pro soccer games, the University of Minnesota football team, spring baseball training for college teams, and every attraction from aerobic dance classes to tractor pulls. The Commission recently purchased a basketball configuration for the stadium and has sights on NCAA tournament games in the near future.

But not all glistens under the Dome. *Chicago Tribune* writer Jon Margolis described the stadium as "an abomination, an affront to taste, humanity, culture, America and, who knows, maybe even the Gods." That unflattering judgment stemmed largely from baseball fans' aversion to the Dome's environmental quirks, among them the lighting, turf, and air patterns, all of which are said to wreak havoc on the game of baseball. Billy Martin, who at the time of this writing was not the manager of the New York Yankees, bemoaned the fact that the 1985 Allstar game was to be played in Minneapolis. "The park," he declared after his team lost several games to the Twins, "should be banned from baseball."

While there are some Minnesota sports fans who share Martin's hostility, for the most part Minnesotans have adapted — however grudgingly — to their new indoor stadium. Although tail-gating is now almost extinct, Minneapolis offers a much larger choice of pre- and post-game night life than Bloomington's hotel lounges ever did.

Four years after the fact, the tale of Minnesota's struggle over a stadium has lost little of its fascination to outsiders weighing decisions involving prospective stadiums. Several cities are now debating whether to build domed stadiums, among them Buffalo, Chicago, San Francisco, Cleveland, Milwaukee, Toronto, New York, and St. Louis. Domes similar in structure to the metrodome have already been built in Syracuse, Vancouver and Indianapolis.

In Minnesota the same two forces at war in the stadium project — Minneapolis and Bloomington — are currently battling over the building of a "Megamall" which Bloomington wants to construct on the old Met stadium site. Minneapolis has opposed the mall, a project which could include hundreds of shops, offices, a convention center, and even amusement rides, on the grounds that it would harm local retail business. A convention center, the downtown forces say, like a stadium, belongs in the city.

But the story's relevance is not limited to domed stadiums or even to Minnesota politics. The conflict between city and suburb, and the controversies over public subsidies for private projects, are part of America's social, political, and economic mix. And the tale of this project's success, of its initial construction and continued economic viability remains a lesson in the art of forging partnerships between business and government.

*Amy Klobuchar is a lawyer in Minneapolis, Minnesota. She is a graduate of Yale University and The University of Chicago Law School.* Uncovering the Dome *was her senior essay at Yale. Her interests include politics, mountain travel, and long-distance bicycling, in which she is sometimes accompanied by her father, Minneapolis* Star *and* Tribune *columnist Jim Klobuchar. She once defined exhaustion as a ten-day 1,000 mile bike ride from Minneapolis to the Teton Mountains. She has since sat in on three-hour arguments over the Metrodome and has changed her mind.*

# FOOTNOTES

## Introduction

1. City Councilman Joseph Strauss quoted in "Downtown Woos Vikings with Promise of Home," Minneapolis *Tribune,* 3 Oct. 1971.
2. Interview with Harvey MacKay, January 11, 1982.
3. Interview with Robert Benedict, January 6, 1982.
4. Interview with Steve Keefe, December 30, 1981.
5. Interview with Louis DeMars, January 5, 1982.
6. For an overview of definitions, see Virginia Held, *The Public Interest and Individual Interests* (New York: Basic Books Inc. 1970). Held arranges public interest theories into three groups: "preponderance theories," "the public interest as common interest," and "unitary conceptions." In summarizing the numerous definitions of the concept I have adopted her framework.
7. Brian Barry, *Political Argument* (New York: Humanities Press, 1965), pg. 207.
8. Ibid., pg. 190.
9. Jean Jacques Rousseau, *Social Contract* (New York: Hafner, 1947), Book II, Chpt. 1, pg. 23. Quoted by Virginia Held, *The Public Interest and Individual Interests,* pg. 102.
10. Jeremy Bentham, *An Introduction to the Principles of Morals and Legislation* (New York: Hafner, 1948), pg. 3. Quoted by Held, pg. 64.
11. Richard E. Flathman, *The Public Interest: An Essay Concerning the Normative Discourse of Politics* (New York: Wiley, 1966), pg. 67.
12. Aristotle, *The Politics of Aristotle* (New York: Oxford University Press, 1962) pg. 1282b. Quoted by Held, pg. 141-142.

13. Felix Frankfurter, *Felix Frankfurter Reminisces,* ed. Harlan B. Phillips (1960) pg. 72.

14. Flathman, pg. 82.

15. In the first six chapters I have adopted an analytical model similar to the model put forth in Graham Allison's study of the Cuban Missile Crisis, *Essence of Decision* (Boston: Little Brown and Company, 1971). Chapters I and II present the government as a "unitary actor," corresponding to Allison's Model 1. In Chapters III and IV, the outcome of the dispute is viewed in terms of patterns of influence, as in Model 2. The behavior of individual decision-makers — how individual perceptions, motivations and "public interest" conceptions determine a policy outcome — is emphasized in chapters V and VI (Allison's Model 3).

## 1. The Stadium: 1971-1973

1. Bill Hengen, "Winter Says Vikings' Road to Glory's an Ego Trip, Too," Minneapolis *Star,* 4 Aug. 1981.

2. Interview with Mike Lynn, August 24, 1981.

3. Quoted by Hengen, Minneapolis *Star,* 4 Aug. 1981.

4. Interview with Clark Griffith, August 28, 1981.

5. Quoted by Beth Reiber, "Minneapolis: A City for the Good Life," Boston *Globe,* 3 Jan. 1982, p. A41.

6. David Walechinsky, Amy Wallace, and Irving Wallace, *The Book of Predictions* (New York: Bantam Books, 1981), p. 3.

7. Interview with Arthur Naftalin, December 28, 1981.

8. Interview with David Roe, August 26, 1981.

9. Quoted by Thomas J. Abercrombie, "A Tale of Twin Cities," *National Geographic,* Nov. 1980, p. 666.

10. Finlay Lewis, *Mondale, Portrait of an American Politician* (New York: Harper & Row, 1980), pg. 48.

11. Interview with Arthur Naftalin.

12. Quoted by Dan Wascoe Jr., "Downtown Woos Vikings with Promise of Home," Minneapolis *Tribune,* 3 Oct. 1971, p. 1a.

13. Interview with David Roe.

14. Ibid.

15. Jim Shoop, "Domed City Grid Stadium Proposed," Minneapolis *Star,* 22 Oct. 1970, pg. 1a.

16. Quoted by Joe Rigert, "A Downtown Football Stadium: Asset or Burden?," Minneapolis *Tribune,* 9 June 1971.

17. Quoted by Deborah Howell, "Next Stadium Step: Check Reaction — City Economic Boom Forecast," Minneapolis *Star,* 13 Jan. 1972.

18. Rigert, "Minneapolis Stadium: Asset or Burden?" Minneapolis *Tribune,* 9 June 1971.

19. Dick Gordon, "St. Paul Proposes Stadium at Fairgrounds," Minneapolis *Star,* 23 Aug. 1972.

20. Jim Klobuchar, "A Stadium for Each of Us," Minneapolis *Star,* 5 Feb. 1972.

21. Dick Gordon and Eric Pianin, "Thompson: Stadium Deadline Jan. 1,"

Minneapolis *Star,* 8 Jan. 1972. p. 14b.
22. Quoted in "Points of Agreement on Downtown Stadium," Minneapolis *Tribune.*
23. Ibid.
24. Dennis Cassano "Businessmen may Subsidize Proposed Downtown Stadium," Minneapolis *Tribune,* 15 Dec. 1972.
25. Cassano, "Businessmen may Subsidize . . ."
26. Cassano, "Businessmen may Subsidize . . ."
27. Quoted by Kathleen Teltsch, "Minnesota a Model of Corporate Aid to Cities," New York *Times,* 27 July 1981.
28. Ibid.
29. Interview with John Cowles Jr., January 8, 1982.
30. Interview with Steve Keefe, December 30, 1981.
31. Ibid.
32. Interview with John Cowles Jr.
33. Ibid.
34. Eric Pianin, "Stadium Gets a Boost with Pledge Report," Minneapolis *Star,* 13 March 1973.
35. Interview with Arthur Naftalin.
36. Interview with Louis DeMars.
37. "Most Oppose Downtown Dome," Minneapolis *Star,* 22 Feb. 1972.
38. "Downtown Stadium Opposed 2-1," Minneapolis *Star,* 12 Dec. 1972.
39. Quoted by Dennis Cassano, "Spannaus: Charter change needed for football stadium referendum," Minneapolis *Tribune,* 28 Sept. 1972.
40. Interview with Louis DeMars.
41. Interview with David Roe.
42. Alan A. Altshuler, *The City Planning Process,* (Ithaca, N.Y.: Cornell University Press, 1965) pg. 190.
43. Alan A. Altshuler, "A Report on the Politics of Minneapolis," (Cambridge, Mass.: Joint Center for Urban Studies of MIT and Harvard University, 1959) Sec. II. pp. 14-15. Quoted by Demetrios Caraley, *City Government and Urban Problems* (Englewood Cliffs, N.J.: Prentice-Hall, 1977), pg. 209.
44. Interview with Arthur Naftalin.
45. Interview with David Roe.
46. Quoted by Nick Coleman, "Stadium Apparently is Dead," Minneapolis *Tribune,* 31 March, 1973.

## 2. A Government Responds

1. Quoted by Arthur T. Johnson, "Congress and Professional Sports: 1951-1978," *Annals of the American Academy of Political and Social Science,* Vol. 445. September, 1979. p. 115.
2. Ibid. p. 102.
3. Quoted by Joseph Durso, *The All-American Dollar: The Big Business of Sports* (Boston: Houghton Mifflin, 1971) pg. 278.
4. Henry Demmert, *The Economics of Professional Team Sports* (Lexington, Mass.: Lexington Books, 1973) pg. 3. (Demmert's book was written in

1973, before soccer was a major league sport).

5. "Will the Raiders be Ruled Out of Bounds?" *Business Week,* 31 March 1980, pg. 46.

6. Quoted by David S. Davenport, "Collusive Competition in Major League Baseball," *American Economist* (Fall, 1969) p. 11.

7. Henry Demmert, pg. 41.

8. Roger Noll quoted in "Pro Sports — Should Government Intervene?" A Public Policy Forum, (Washington: The American Enterprise Institute for Public Policy Research, 1977) p. 6.

9. There are some exceptions to this rule (i.e. Texas Stadium in Dallas and Dodger Stadium in Los Angeles).

10. Quoted by Michael Roberts, *Fans — How We Go Crazy over Sports* (Washington: The New Republic Book Co., 1976) pg. 137.

11. Quoted in "Downtown Woos Vikings . . ." Minneapolis *Tribune.*

12. Charles Maher, "Major Sports Stadiums: They Keep Going Up," Los Angeles *Times,* 14 Nov. 1971.

13. Benjamin Okner, "Subsidies of Sports Arenas," in *Government and the Sports Business,* ed. Roger Noll (Washington D.C.: Brookings Institution, 1974) p. 326.

14. Ibid., pg. 325.

15. Quoted in "Stadiums: City Status Symbol," *Newsweek* No. 62, 30 Sept. 1963, pg. 75.

16. "Superdome has Super Money Troubles," *Business Week,* 24 May 1976, pg. 42.

17. Quoted by Charles Burck, "The Superstadium Game," *Fortune,* March, 1973, pg. 178.

18. Okner, pg. 347.

19. Quoted in "Will the Raiders be Ruled Out of Bounds," *Business Week,* 31 March 1981, pg. 46.

20. Okner, pg. 332.

21. Ibid. pg. 332.

22. "It's Have Team, Will Travel in Pro Football," *Wall Street Journal,* 23 July 1980, pg. 22 Col. 4.

23. Quoted by Joseph Durso, *The All-American Dollar: The Big Business of Sports,* (Boston: Houghton Mifflin, 1971). pg. 126.

24. "It's Have Team, Will Travel . . ." *Wall Street Journal.*

25. "Will the Raiders be Ruled . . ." *Business Week.*

26. Mancur Olson, *The Logic of Collective Action,* (Boston: Harvard University Press, 1971) pp. 14-15.

27. For a critical assessment of these claims see Benjamin Okner, pgs. 328-330. Okner states that when measuring the economic revenue generated by a stadium, "one should take account only of the *marginal* or *extra revenue* that would not be collected by the city in the absence of the facility."

28. Quoted by Howell, "Next Stadium Step . . ."

29. Doane, D.P., "Impact of the Baseball Strike," *U.S. News,* No. 90, 29 June 1981, pg. 64.

30. Interview with Dave Roe.

31. Interview with Harvey MacKay.
32. Quoted by Michael Roberts, *Fans,* pg. 138.
33. Interview with MacKay.
34. Edward C. Banfield and James Q. Wilson, *City Politics,* (Cambridge, Mass.: Harvard University Press, 1963), pg. 18.
35. Demetrios Caraley, *City Government and Urban Problems* (Englewood Cliffs, N.J.: Prentice-Hall, 1977).
36. Banfield and Wilson, pg. 58.
37. Interview with Arthur Naftalin.
38. John Bainbridge, *The Super-Americans* (Garden City N.Y.: Doubleday, 1961).
39. Quoted by J. Anthony Lukas, "Wanta Buy Two Seats for the Dallas Cowboys?" *Esquire* September, 1972. pg. 122.
40. Quoted in "New York City to Buy Yankee Stadium, Seen as Vital Cultural Need," *Wall Street Journal,* March 3, 1971, pg. 13, Col. 1.
41. Robert Lipsyte, "A Diamond in the Ashes," *Sports Illustrated,* April 26, 1976, pg. 43.

## 3. The Stadium: 1973-1977

1. Quoted by Betty Wilson, "Stadium Still Dead Despite City Hall Shift," Minneapolis *Star,* 9 Nov. 1973.
2. Interview with Arthur Naftalin.
3. Interview with Steve Keefe.
4. Quoted by Dick Gordon, "Rozelle Won't Order Bigger Stadium . . . but," Minneapolis *Star,* 31 Dec. 1974.
5. Interview with Harvey MacKay.
6. Quoted by Tom Davies, Minneapolis *Tribune,* 21 Feb. 1982.
7. Ibid.
8. Interview with John Cowles Jr.
9. Ibid.
10. Interview with Harvey MacKay.
11. Ibid. Considering the Vikings abysmal Super Bowl performances (with four embarrassing losses they have acquired the reputation as the "team that can never win the big one") skeptics tend to disagree with MacKay's claim that the use of the state's name in this context was "positive" advertising.
12. Interview with Senator Jack Davies.
13. Patrick Marx, "Five Stadium Options Offered," Minneapolis *Star,* 21 Dec. 1974.
14. Quoted by Sue Chastain, "Bloomington to Detail Latest Stadium Proposal with Gusto," Minneapolis *Star,* 6 Sept. 1974.
15. Quoted by Betty Wilson, "Governor Says Stadium Needed to Keep Teams," Minneapolis *Star,* 9 April 1975.
16. Quoted by Betty Wilson, "Senate Study Doubts Dome Proposal Data," Minneapolis *Star,* 10 March 1975.
17. Quoted by Betty Wilson, "Panel Buries Stadium Bills in Study Plan," Minneapolis *Star,* 10 April 1975.

18. Quoted by Peter Vanderpoel, "Vikings Say Stadium Size Hurts Profits," Minneapolis *Tribune*, April, 1975.
19. Interview with Mike Lynn.
20. Interview with Clark Griffith.
21. Quoted by Jim Klobuchar, "Offer from Rams Owner," Minneapolis *Star*, 21 Dec. 1976.
22. Interview with Mike Lynn.
23. Quoted by Eric Pianin and Richard Gibson, "Grant Adds his Weight to Pleas for Stadium," Minneapolis *Star*, 5 Feb. 1976.
24. Interview with Mike Lynn.
25. Interview with Robert Benedict.
26. "Minnesotans Fear Loss of Pro Teams if No Stadium Built," Minneapolis *Tribune*, 24 March 1976.
27. Interview with Clark Griffith.
28. Interview with Mike Lynn.
29. Interview with Steve Keefe.
30. Quoted in "Vikings Willing to Listen to Offer," Minneapolis *Star*, 19 March 1976.
31. Interview with Dave Roe.
32. Ibid.
33. Quoted by David Kuhn, "Stadium Bill Apparently Dead," Minneapolis *Tribune*, 18 March 1976.
34. Representative John Biersdorf, Quoted in "Lack of Interest in Stadium," Minneapolis *Star*.
35. Quoted by Jim Klobuchar, "Would You Get Lost in Granite Falls?" Minneapolis *Star*.
36. Interview with Steve Keefe.
37. Interview with Louis DeMars.
38. Senator Robert North, Quoted by David Kuhn, "Stadium Bill Apparently Dead," Minneapolis *Tribune*, 18 March 1976.
39. Quoted by David Kuhn and Dennis Cassano, "Senate Passes Bill for Stadium Rebate," Minneapolis *Tribune* 4 April 1976.
40. Quoted by Eric Pianin, "House Won't Consider Senate Tax Bill to Merge Stadium, Rebate Plans," Minneapolis *Star*, 5 April 1976.
41. Ibid.
42. Interview with Steve Keefe.
43. Quoted by Allan Holbert, "Site-Neutral Stadium Bill is Presented in Legislature," Minneapolis *Tribune*, 10 March 1977.
44. Interview with Steve Keefe.
45. Quoted by Blair Charnley and Betty Wilson, "Legislators Preparing Covered-Stadium Bill that Doesn't Specify Site or Design," Minneapolis *Star*, 14 Jan. 1977.
46. Interview with Robert Benedict.
47. Interview with Jack Davies.
48. See appendix.
49. Quoted in "Perpich Signs Stadium Bill," Minneapolis *Tribune*, 17 May 1977.

## 4. The Interest Group Battle

1. Senator Steve Keefe, Interview.
2. Although the issue was aired at the state rather than local level, many of the formal and informal characteristics of Minneapolis government outlined in chapters I and II, such as the "good government" political culture and the civic-minded "business tradition," also apply to the state government.
3. The former analysis corresponds to Graham Allison's "Model 1," the latter "Model 2."
4. Flathman, pg. 69.
5. Olson, pg. 7.
6. Banfield, *Political Influence*, pg. 3.
7. Interview with Robert Benedict.
8. Interview with Robert Benedict.
9. Interview with John Cowles Jr.
10. Interview with Dave Roe.
11. Floyd Hunter, *Community Power Structure*, (Chapel Hill: University of North Carolina Press, 1953). pp. 101-102.
12. Ibid.
13. Interview with John Cowles Jr.
14. Ibid.
15. Caraley, pg. 300.
16. Robert Dahl, *Who Governs* (New Haven: Yale University Press, 1961), pg. 72.
17. Because of the confusion which characterized the issue, it is impossible to verify this statement. The passage of the no-site bill may indicate that it is a possible interpretation, however.

## 5. The Stadium: 1977-1978

1. Interview with Solveig Premack, January 4, 1982.
2. Interview with Solveig Premack.
3. Interview with Governor Perpich, August 25, 1981.
4. Interview with Solveig Premack.
5. Interview with Dan Brutger, January 7, 1982.
6. Interview with Solveig Premack.
7. Interview with Kelly Gage, January 4, 1982.
8. Interview with Kelly Gage.
9. Ibid.
10. Interview with Governor Perpich.
11. Ibid.
12. Ibid.
13. Interview with Dan Brutger.
14. Interview with Governor Perpich.
15. Commissioner Kennon was active in the first, Commissioner Gornick in the second.
16. Ibid.

17. Mayor Phil Cohen, quoted by Robin Finn, "Brutger and Poss — the Masons of the Metrodome," Minneapolis *Star*, 18 Dec. 1980.
18. Interview with Don Poss.
19. Interview with Don Poss.
20. Quoted by Mike Norton, "Oh Give Me a Home where a Stadium Roams," Minneapolis *Tribune*, 22 June 1977.
21. Quoted by Peter Ackerberg, "Residents Fight Site for Domed Stadium," Minneapolis *Star*, 7 July 1977.
22. Interview with Dan Brutger.
23. "Bond Limits 'too low' to Build Dome," Minneapolis *Star*, 28 Sept. 1978.
24. Interview with Solveig Premack.
25. Interview with Don Poss.
26. Interview with Don Poss.
27. Interview with Solveig Premack.
28. Interview with Solveig Premack.
29. Interview with Kelly Gage.
30. Quoted by Kathe Wingert, "Citizens' Group Tries to 'Save the Met,' " *Minnesota Daily*, 2 Oct. 1978.
31. "77% Support a New Stadium," Minneapolis *Tribune*, 16 April 1978. This positive support for a new stadium might have stemmed from the questions which proceeded the "worthwhile project" question. First, those questioned were asked whether Minnesota gained from having pro sports. Secondly they were asked whether or not they considered themselves sports fans. 93% believed that the state gained from having pro sports. 66% considered themselves sports fans.
32. "42% No, 38% Yes," Minneapolis *Tribune*, 26 Nov. 1978.
33. Interview with Mike Lynn.
34. Interview with Solveig Premack.
35. Interview with Kelly Gage.
36. Interview with Dan Brutger.
37. Interview with John Cowles Jr.
38. Ibid.
39. Ibid.
40. Quoted by Robert Guenther and Robert Whereatt, "The Stadium: Why? Where? How? If?" Minneapolis *Star*, 27 Nov. 1978.
41. Cowles, Quoted by Robert Guenther, "Downtown Site-Buying Scheme Ready," Minneapolis *Star* 28 Sept. 1978.
42. Interview with Charles Krusell.
43. Quoted by Robert Guenther and Robert Whereatt, "The Stadium: Why? Where? . . ." Minneapolis *Star*.
44. Robert Whereatt, "Millions Pledged for City Stadium," Minneapolis *Star*, 15 Nov. 1978.
45. Interview with Dan Brutger.
46. Interview with Solveig Premack.
47. Quoted by Robert Whereatt, "Stadium Clock Winds Down as Rivals Go For Extra Points," Minneapolis *Star*, 16 Nov. 1978.
48. Ibid.

49. Quoted by Robert Whereatt, "Planner is for New Football Park, Met Fix-up," Minneapolis *Star,* 15 Aug. 1978.
50. Ibid.
51. Quoted by Max Nichols, "Winter: Vikings Need a Cover," Minneapolis *Star,* 30 Aug. 1978.
52. Quoted by Max Nichols, "Winter, 'I Don't Intend to Move,' " Minneapolis *Star* 18 Aug. 1978.
53. Quoted in "Pro Teams Give Views on Stadium," Minneapolis *Tribune,* 23 Nov. 1978.
54. Ibid.
55. Jim Klobuchar, "Mike Lynn Rattles Our Minds," Minneapolis *Star,* 24 Nov. 1978.
56. Interview with Dan Brutger.
57. Quoted in "Panel Picks Downtown Site," Minneapolis *Tribune,* 2 Dec. 1978.
58. Ibid.

## 6. Politics and the Public Interest

1. Interview with Steve Keefe.
2. Interview with Dan Brutger.
3. Ibid.
4. Interview with Don Poss.
5. Interview with Solveig Premack.
6. Interview with Dan Brutger.
7. Edward Banfield, *Political Influence,* pg. 330.
8. Interview with Solveig Premack.
9. Interview with Dan Brutger.
10. Interview with Kelly Gage.
11. Interview with Robert Benedict.
12. Interview with Kelly Gage.
13. Quoted by Robert Whereatt, "Planner is for . . ." Minneapolis *Star.*
14. Interview with Solveig Premack.
15. Interview with Governor Perpich.
16. Interview with Dan Brutger.
17. Ibid.
18. Brutger's site selection statement.

## 7. The Stadium: 1979-1982

1. Quoted by Patrick Marx, "Repeal is Tough Test for Stadium Backers," Minneapolis *Star,* Jan. 25, 1979.
2. Quoted by Todd Glasenapp, "Possible Cost Overruns Lead Legislators to Oppose Stadium," *Minnesota Daily,* 24 Jan. 1979.
3. Quoted by Jim Shoop and Robert Whereatt, "The Doom that Befell the Dome," Minneapolis *Star,* 11 April 1979.
4. Quoted in "Stadium Panel Member Assails Liquor Tax Foes," Minneapolis *Tribune,* 15 Feb. 1979.
5. Interview with Steve Keefe.
6. Quoted by Lori Sturdevant, "One Strike Against the Stadium, and It's

the House's Turn to Pitch,'' Minneapolis *Tribune,* 16 Feb. 1979.

7. Quoted by Lori Sturdevant, "These Folks are Really Against the Stadium," Minneapolis *Tribune,* 7 March 1979.
8. Ibid.
9. Ibid.
10. Senator George Perpich, Quoted by Lori Sturdevant, "One Strike Against, . . ." Minneapolis *Tribune.*
11. Fraser is now Mayor of Minneapolis.
12. Quoted by Patrick Marx, "Repeal is Tough Test for Stadium Backers," Minneapolis *Star,* 25 Jan. 1979.
13. Interview with John Cowles Jr.
14. Quoted by Ruth Hamel, "Star, Trib Staffs Fear Credibility Loss Over Stadium," *Minnesota Daily,* 1 March, 1979.
15. Ibid.
16. Jon Kerr, letter to Cameron Blodgett, Executive Secretary, Minnesota Press Council, March 6, 1979.
17. Quoted by Lori Sturdevant, "These Folks . . ." Minneapolis *Tribune.*
18. Representative Roger Laufenburger of Lewiston, Quoted by Lori Sturdevant, "One Strike Against the Stadium . . ." Minneapolis *Tribune.*
19. Quoted by Robert Whereatt, "Stadium Still on Obstacle Course," Minneapolis *Star.*
20. Quoted by Max Nichols, "A Mood of Destruction," Minneapolis *Star,* 9 Feb. 1979.
21. Quoted by Robert Whereatt, "Downtown Dome is Wounded; But is it Dead?" Minneapolis *Star,* 9 Feb. 1979.
22. Quoted by Jim Shoop, "Quie to Kill Liquor Tax Bill," Minneapolis *Star,* 9 April 1979.
23. Interview with Mike Lynn.
24. Ibid.
25. Ibid.
26. Quoted by Lori Sturdevant, "No Dome May Mean No Free City Land," Minneapolis *Tribune,* 26 April 1979.
27. Ibid.
28. Interview with Mike Lynn.
29. Representative Ray Faricy, Quoted by Robert Whereatt, "Stadium on Road to Limbo After House Vote," Minneapolis *Star,* 21 May 1979.
30. Quoted by Lori Sturdevant, "House Adopts Stadium Bill," Minneapolis *Tribune,* 22 May 1979.
31. Quoted by Lori Sturdevant, "House Panel Backs Altered Stadium Bill," Minneapolis *Tribune,* 11 May 1979.
32. Interview with Don Poss.
33. Quoted by Lori Sturdevant, "Is Calvin Griffith a Business Genius or a Feudal Flop?" Minneapolis *Tribune,* 21 Aug. 1979.
34. Ibid.
35. Quoted by Lori Sturdevant, "Coleman to Fight Stadium Decisions in Court," Minneapolis *Tribune,* 24 Aug. 1979.
36. Ibid.
37. Charles Whiting, "Your guess: What does Coleman Want?"

Minneapolis *Star,* 4 Sept. 1979.
38. Interview with Robert Ashbach.
39. Interview with Steve Keefe.
40. Interview with Jack Davies.
41. Ibid.
42. Interview with Don Poss.
43. Ibid.
44. Ibid.
45. Ibid.
46. Interview with Kelly Gage.
47. Interview with Dan Brutger.
48. Interview with Dan Brutger.
49. Interview with Solveig Premack.
50. Interview with Dan Brutger.
51. Interview with Dan Brutger.
52. Interview with Don Poss.
53. Interview with Robert Benedict.
54. Interview with Don Poss.
55. Interview with Don Poss.
56. Interview with Mike Lynn.
57. Interview with Don Poss.
58. Interview with John Cowles Jr.
59. Ibid.
60. Interview with Don Poss.
61. Jeff Brown, "The Dome Deal: City Gave Developers Rights to 50-Block Area," Minneapolis *Star,* 9 Oct. 1981.
62. Ibid.
63. Tim McGuire, "Dome Report Put Star Through the Wringer," Minneapolis *Star,* 9 Oct. 1981.

## 8. From the Capitol to the Cogwheels

1. Interview with Kelly Gage.
2. Jeffrey L. Pressman and Aaron Wildavsky, *Implementation* (Berkeley: University of California Press, 1973), pg. 94.
3. Steve Keefe, Interview.
4. Representative Roger Laufenburger of Lewiston, Quoted by Lori Sturdevant, "One Strike Against the Stadium . . ." Minneapolis *Tribune.*
5. Pressman and Wildavsky, pg. 92.
6. Quoted in "Stadium Panel Member Assails . . ." Minneapolis *Tribune.*
7. Pressman and Wildavsky, pg. 90.
8. Theodore Lowi, *The End of Liberalism,* (New York: Norton, 1969) pg. 311.

## Conclusion

1. Interview with Louis DeMars.
2. Interview with Arthur Naftalin.
3. Interview with Louis DeMars.

# BIBLIOGRAPHY

Allison, Graham. *Essence of Decision: Explaining the Cuban Missile Crisis.* Boston: Little, Brown, and Co., 1971.

Altshuler, Alan A. *The City Planning Process.* Ithaca: Cornell Univ. Press, 1965.

Altshuler, Alan A. "A Report on the Politics of Minneapolis." Cambridge, Mass.: Center for Urban Studies, MIT and Harvard, 1959.

Aristotle. *The Politics of Aristotle.* New York: Oxford University Press, 1962.

Banfield, Edward C. and James Q. Wilson. *City Politics.* Cambridge, Mass.: Harvard Univ. Press, 1963.

Banfield, Edward. *Political Influence.* New York: The Free Press of Glencoe, 1961.

Barry, Brian. *Political Argument.* New York: Humanities Press, 1965.

Bentham, Jeremy. *An Introduction to the Principles of Morals and Legislation.* New York: Hafner, 1948.

Burck, Charles. "The Superstadium Game." *Fortune,* March, 1973, pp. 104-7.

Caraley, Demetrios. *City Government and Urban Problems.* Englewood Cliffs, N.J.: Prentice-Hall, 1977.

Dahl, Robert. *Who Governs.* New Haven: Yale Univ. Press, 1961.

Davenport, David S. "Collusive Competition in Major League Baseball." *American Economist,* Fall, 1969, pp. 6-30.

Demmert, Henry S. *Economics of Professional Team Sports.* Lexington, Mass.: Lexington Books, 1973.

Doane, D.P. "Impact of the Baseball Strike." *U.S. News,* 29 June 1981, pg. 64.

Durso, Joseph, *The All-American Dollar: The Big Business of Sports.* Boston:

# BIBLIOGRAPHY

Houghton Mifflin, 1971.

Flathman, Richard E. *The Public Interest: An Essay Concerning the Normative Discourse of Politics.* New York: Wiley, 1966.

Held, Virginia. *The Public Interest and Individual Interests.* New York: Basic Books, 1970.

Hunter, Floyd. *Community Power Structure.* Chapel Hill: Univ. of North Carolina Press, 1953.

"It's Have Team, Will Travel in Pro Football." *Wall Street Journal,* 23 July 1980, p. 22., col. 4.

Johnson, Arthur T. "Congress and Professional Sports: 1951-1978." *Annals of the American Academy of Political and Social Science,* Vol. 445, Sept. 1979, pp. 102-15.

Lipsyte, Robert. "A Diamond in the Ashes." *Sports Illustrated,* 26 April, 1976, pp. 34-40.

Lowi, Theodore. *The End of Liberalism.* New York: Norton, 1969.

Lucas, Anthony, "Wanta Buy Two Seats for the Dallas Cowboys?" *Esquire* Sept., 1972, pp. 121-4.

"New York City to Buy Yankee Stadium." *Wall Street Journal,* 3 March 1971, p. 13, Col. 1.

Noll, Roger, ed. *Government and the Sports Business.* Washington D.C.: Brookings Institution, 1974.

Olson, Mancur. *The Logic of Collective Action.* Boston: Harvard Univ. Press, 1971.

Okner, Benjamin. "Subsidies of Sports Arenas." *In Government and the Sports Business.* Ed. Roger Noll. Washington D.C.: Brookings Institution, 1974, pp. 325-47.

Pressman, Jeffrey L. and Aaron Wildavsky. *Implementation.* Berkeley: Univ. of Calf. Press, 1973.

"Pro Sports: Should Government Intervene?" A Public Policy Forum. Washington: *The American Enterprise Institute for Public Policy Research,* 1977.

Roberts, Michael. *Fans: How We Go Crazy over Sports.* Washington: The New Republic Book Co., 1976.

Rousseau, Jean Jacques. *Social Contract.* New York: Hafner, 1947.

"Stadiums: City Status Symbol." *Newsweek* No. 62, 30 Sept. 1963, pp. 34-5.

"Superdome Has Super Money Troubles," *Business Week,* 24 May 1976, p. 42.

"Will the Raiders be Ruled Out of Bounds?" *Business Week,* 31 March 1981, p. 46.